Healthy Recipes

© Copyright 2010 New Century
ISBN 978-1-890035-76-1
Printed 2010

All rights reserved.
Permission is hereby granted to make copies of small parts (not in its entirety) of this document for non-commercial purposes provided the original copyright notice with the author's name is included. No electronic copies of any kind allowed.

Published in the United States by
New Century Press
1055 Bay Blvd., Suite C
Chula Vista, CA 91911
1 800 519-2465
www.newcenturypress.com

Other books by Dr. Clark available from New Century Press:

The Cure For All Cancers
    (English, German, Italian, Mongolian, Russian)
The Cure For All Diseases
    (English, French, German, Hungarian, Italian, Polish, Portuguese/Brazilian, Russian, Serbian, Spanish)
The Cure For All Advanced Cancers
    (English, German, Italian, Russian)
The Cure For HIV And AIDS
    (English)
The Prevention Of All Cancers
    (English, Italian)
Syncrometer® Science Laboratory Manual
    (English, French, Spanish)

The following recipes on food, drink and health improvements are a compilation from Dr. Clark's books:
The Cure For All Cancers
The Cure For HIV And AIDS
The Cure For All Diseases
The Cure For All Advanced Cancers
The Prevention Of All Cancers
The Cure And Prevention Of All Cancers

Contents

Rules for Preparing Recipes 9
Going Shopping 9
Food Treatments 11
Lugol's Food Sanitizer 11
Cysteine-Salt Food Sanitizer 11
HCl Food Sanitizer 11
Full Spectrum Light Food Sanitizer 12
Common Food Rules 12
Food Guidelines 16

Daily Diet 17
Salt 17
Two to One Sodium-Potassium Salt 17
B-C Salt 17
Milk 18
Sweeteners 19
Water 20
Bread 21
Eggs 22
Beans, Dried Peas, Lentils & Rice 23
Meats 23
Fruits & Vegetables 24
Complete Meal Drinks 25
Blended Turkey 27
Blended Stew 28
Beverages 28
Quick Vanilla Drink 28
Quick Almond Drink 28
Four Egg Nogs 29
Cream Shake 29
Coconut Egg Nog 29
Egg Nog Cream Shake 29
Hot Vanilla Milk 30

Lemon / Oil Drink	30
Whole Lemonade	30
Lemonade	31
Watermelon / Banana	31
Melon / Lemon	31
Fresh Pineapple Juice	31
Honeydew Ambrosia	32
Fresh Tomato Juice	32
Almond Milk	33
Coconut Milk	33
Coconut - Tangerine Juice	33
Coconut Smoothie	34
Red Milk	34
Maple Milk Shake	35
Yankee Drink	35
C-Milk	35
Half and Half	35
Cream Shake	35
Raw Certified Milk	35
Baby Coconut Juice	35
Coconut - Tangerine Juice	36
Buttermilk - C I	36
Buttermilk - C II	36
Green Dinosaur	37
Green Goodness	37
Green Drink	38
Barley Water	38
My Own Soda Pop	38
My Own Super C-Pop	39
Zoom Juice	39
Mini - Zoom Juice	40
Nopales Drink	40

Spreads 41

Nearly Butter	41
Butter	41
Real Butter	42
Coconut Butter	42
Spreadable Butter	43
Peanut Butter	43
Preserves	43
Marmalade	44
Kumquat Marmalade	45

Pancakes 45

Maria's Best Pancakes	45

Cereals 46
   Three Granolas 46
   Jump Start Cereal 48
Dressings 48
   C-Dressing 48
   Mom's Mayo 49
   Sour Cream-C 49
   Beet Popsicles 49
   Queen of Hearts Dressing (hides all supplements) 50
Sauces 50
   Tomato Sauce I 50
   Tomato Sauce II 51
   Pasta Pizza Sauce or Red Sauce 51
   Sauce No. I 52
   Sauce No. II 52
   Cheese Sauce 52
   Yogurt & Cottage Cheese 52
   Cottage Cheese "Paneer" 52
   Cottage Cheese "Zuppe" 53
   Fast Food Cottage Cheese 53
   Goat Cheese 53
   Flax Seed 53
Soups 54
   Chicken Broth 54
   Cheese Soup 55
   Bone Marrow-Beef Broth 56
Something Sour 57
   Citric Tangerine Dessert 57
   Lettuce A'la Crème – A TV Snack 57
   Spice Mix 58
   Spice Mix Straight 58
Desserts 58
   Coconut Whipping Cream 58
   Chewy Barley Pearls 58
   Barley Flakes 59
   Tapioca - Barley Pudding 59
   Brazil Nut Split 59
   Santa Split 60
   Baked Apples 60
   Lettuce - Nut Salad 60
   Cottage Cheese Cake 61

- Cold Delights 61
  - 5-Minute Raspberry Ice Cream 61
  - Pear Slush 62
  - 5-Minute Strawberry Ice Cream 63
- Cookies, Cakes & Pies 64
- Teas for Pleasure & Health 65
  - Hydrangea Tea 65
  - Wheat Germ Tea 65
  - Rose Hips Tea 66
  - Burdock Tea 66
  - Coconut Tea 66
  - Eucalyptus Tea 67
  - Bone Healer Tea 68
  - Lung Tea 68
  - Detox-Tea 68
  - Buski Tea 69

Health Recipes 70

- Beverages for Health 70
  - Moose Elm Drink 70
  - Alginate/Intestinal Healer 70
  - Raw Bitters 71
  - Raw Liver Cocktail 71
  - Pomegranate Seed Drink 72
  - Shark Cartilage 72
- Parasite Killer Recipes 73
  - Spice Syrup 73
  - General Spice Syrup Recipe 73
  - Spice Tea 74
  - Prion Punch 75
  - Paragonimus Punch 75
  - Six Fresh Seeds 77
- Parasite-Killing Program 78
  - Parasite Program Handy Chart 81
  - Maintenance Parasite Program 82
- Parasite Essential Foods 83
  - Pet Parasite Program 84
- Organ Improvement Recipes 87
  - Kidney Cleanse 87
  - Liver Herbs 90
  - Liver Cleanse 91

Immunity Boosters 97
- Ferritin Fighter 97
- Dye Remover Syrup 98
- Freon Removal Program 98
- L-A Recipe 99
- L-G Recipe 99

Supplements for Special Purposes 101
- How To Take Supplements 101
- Bloating and Gassiness 102
- Intestinal Blockage or Bleeding 103
- Poor Digestion 103
- Better Digestion 103
- Raw Beet Cocktail 104
- Beet Juice 104
- Diarrhea and Constipation 105
- Bowel Program 105
- Anemia 106
- Insomnia 107
- Lymphoma 107
- Liver Cancer 108
- Bone Cancer 108
- Kill Bacteria 109
- Kill Leftover Pathogens 110
- Kill Adenovirus 112
- Herbal Treatment of Whooping Cough 112
- Kill Tapeworms 113
- Restore Major Minerals 113
- Get The Ammonia Out 114
- Supply Amino Acids 116
- Return Immunity 117
- Bring Back Iron 118
- Remove Calcium Deposits 118
- Digest the Tumor 119

Healthy Helpers 120
Natural Body Product Recipes 120
- Borax Liquid Soap 120
- Laundry 121
- Dishes 121
- Dishwasher 122
- Sink 122
- Shampoo 122
- Baking Soda Shampoo 123

Hair Spray 123
Homemade Soap 124
Liquid Soap 124
Skin Sanitizer 125
Deodorant 125
Brushing Teeth 127
Oregano Oil Toothpowder 128
Denture Cleaner 128
Denture Adhesive 129
Mouthwash 130
Contact Lens Solution 130
Lip Soother 130
Foot Powder 131
Skin Healer Moisturizer Lotion 131
Other Skin Healers 132
Massage Oil 132
Sunscreen Lotion 132
Nose Salve 133
Quick Cornstarch Skin Softener 133
Cornstarch Skin Softener 133
After Shaves 133
Personal Lubricants 134
Baby Wipes 134
People Wipes 134

Natural Cosmetic Recipes 135
Eyeliner and Eyebrow Pencil 135
Lipstick 135
Face Powder 136
Blush 136

Household Product Recipes 136
Floor Cleaner 136
Furniture Duster & Window Cleaner 136
Furniture Polish 137
Insect Killer 137
Ant Repellent 137
Flower & Foliage Spray 137
Herbal Moth Ball Substitute 138
Carpet Cleaner 138

Sources 139

Rules for Preparing Recipes

Going Shopping

Shop for kosher foods whenever possible. Search for these symbols: K, U. Shop for Asian imports. This still does not guarantee their safety. Don't shop for anything in glass bottles unless you can test for thallium. That is a major seeped metal from both amber and clear glass, besides Teflon. If your legs ache be extra careful.

Organic produce has much less dye and pesticide pollution than regular produce, but buy it only if the local water, used to spray on the shelf for freshness, is not the chlorox bleach kind. Find a store with safe water by testing it for chlorox. Asbestos tufts adhering to the outside of foods is just as severe a problem with organic produce. When I tested some farmers' market produce, it was free of asbestos. Search for <u>organic produce at farmers' markets</u>. Potatoes and sweet potatoes not sprayed against sprouting or greased against wilting, would be a rare find. The others have malonic acid deep inside. Next best might be a small corner grocery store. Ask which day their produce arrives to get it fresh.

No foods are safe, though, unless cleaned up with hot-washes and sterilized. Do not buy a spray that removes spray, either; the one I tested had more solvents than the original sprayed food. A UV lamp is the handiest for sterilizing fresh vegetables that have already been tested for chlorox and thallium.

Choose your recipes carefully. Feel free to vary them.

KOSHER FOODS ARE AN EXCEPTION
Most foods labeled kosher had no asbestos, azo dyes, lanthanides, heavy metals, acrylic acid, or urethane. They did not even have rabbit fluke! Does this reflect on superior sanitation or quality control? Or some mystery-method? How do they do it?

Recently many new Asian and kosher foods have reached the marketplace, including bottled water. Choose kosher foods to avoid chlorination. Make a list of safe foods for your area. Here are some kosher symbols. Look on the internet for more.

Food Treatments

1. Sterilize every item before or after preparation. It only needs to be done once.
2. Use stove top, not microwave, to protect germanium and vitamin C.

Lugol's Food Sanitizer

- 1 drop Lugol's iodine solution
- 1 quart/L water

Fill sink or bowl with the measured amount of water. Draw a line here, so future treatments do not require measuring the water. Add Lugol's (1 drop per quart). Dip lettuce and spinach so leaves are well wetted for one minute! Rinsing is optional. Do not save the water for later use — it will lose its potency.

Cysteine-Salt Food Sanitizer

- $1/8$ teaspoon cysteine powder
- $1/8$ teaspoon salt
- 1 quart/L water

Stir to dissolve. Immerse produce for five minutes. No need to rinse.

When cysteine-salt is used to sterilize a beverage, such as milk or juice, it soon becomes sulfurous, so use beverage immediately.

HCl Food Sanitizer

- 1-2 drops per cup water

Agitate food well. Let stand several minutes.

Healthy Recipes

Full Spectrum Light Food Sanitizer

Wet foods need 5 minutes; dry foods need 20 minutes. Place within inches of the bulb.

Common Food Rules

FRUITS	has asbestos	has dye	has benzene (pesticide)	has mold	dip in HCl (2 d/ cup to serving)	add HCl (to serving)	add B2
			Y = Yes or N = No				
Apples, kiwi, pears, peaches. Soak twice in hot water for 1 minute, dry, cut out stem and flower ends deeply.	Y	Y	Y	N	Y	Y	Y
Avocado, banana. Soak twice in hot water, dry.	Y	Y	Y	N	N	Y	N
Canned fruit	Y	Impossible to remove asbestos. Avoid.					
Cherries and most berries	N	N	Y	Y	Y	Y	Y
Coconut, fresh. Remove brown skin from pieces.	N	N	N	N	Y	N	N
Currants, raisins, other dried fruit	Y	Can't be washed off. Avoid.					
Grapes, strawberries		Avoid, too moldy.					
Grapefruit, lemons, pomegranates. Soak in hot water twice and dry.	N	Y	Y	N	N	Y	N
Pineapple. Wash and drain. Peel very thickly so no "eyes" are left.	N	N	Y	N	N	Y	Y
Plums, kumquats, nectarines. Soak in hot water twice for 1 minute, cut out stem widely.	Y	N	Y	Y	N	Y	Y

HEALTHY RECIPES 13

	has asbestos	has dye	has benzene (pesticide)	has mold	dip in HCl (2 d/ cup	add HCl (to serving)	add B2
GRAINS							
Breads	N	Y	Y	Y	N	Y	N
Buckwheat, Kamut, oats, quinoa, millet, cornmeal, cream of wheat, grits, rice. Wash three times and drain to remove asbestos. Cook twice.	Y	Y	Y	Y	Y	Y	Y
Flaxseed	N	N	Y	Y	Y	Y	Y
Flour, white and bleached.	N	N	N	N	N	N	N
Sunflower seeds	Y	Too difficult to remove asbestos. Avoid.					
Wheat berries	Y	Too difficult to remove asbestos.					
VEGETABLES							
Artichokes. Cook twice.	N	N	Y	Y	Y	Y	Y
Beets, radishes (raw). Wash, dry. Peel the top half first so no dirt or fingers touch clean part.	N	N	Y	N	Y	Y	Y
Canned vegetables	Too many chemicals. Avoid.						
Chilies, peppers; hot soak twice.	Y	N	Y	N	Y	Y	Y
Corn in husk, cut away tip if exposed.	N	N	N	N	N	N	N
Dried beans, Adzuki, pinto, soy, garbanzo, split peas, lentils. Wash several times to remove asbestos. Use pressure cooker; cook twice.	Y	Y	Y	Y	Y	Y	Y
Eggplant, cucumber; hot wash twice, peel.	N	Y	Y	N	N	Y	N

HEALTHY RECIPES   14

	has asbestos	has dye	has benzene (pesticide)	has mold	dip in HCl (2 d/ cup	add HCl (to serving)	add B2
Cooked greens, incl. beet tops, cauliflower, collards, cabbage, kale, Swiss chard, green beans. Wash twice in hot water. Cook twice.	Y	Y	Y	N	Y	Y	N
Raw greens, lettuce, spinach, parsley. Soak in hot water twice, shaking between soaks. Sterilize in cold HCl-water.	Y	Y	Y	N	Y	Y	N
Mushrooms	Too difficult to sterilize, don't use.						
Nuts, in the shell only. Remove brown skins.	Y	N	Y	Y	Y	Y	Y
Onions, garlic, leeks. Peel apart. Hot soak twice; then HCl-water.	N	N	Y	N	Y	Y	N
Peanut butter	N	Y	Y	Y	N	Y	Y
Potatoes, red and white. Hot soak twice. Peel.	Y	Y	Y	Y	Y	Y	Y
Potatoes, brown	Has too much zearalenone throughout. Avoid.						
Squash, incl. butternut, zucchini. Soak in hot water twice and dry. Peel if possible.	N	Y	Y	N	N	Y	N
Tapioca	?	Y	Y	Y	Y	Y	Y
DAIRY (HCl is added while stirring)							
Butter. Let soften. Add B2 and HCl, whip. Refrigerate.	N	Y	Y	N	N	4 per ¼ lb.	Y
Buttermilk	N	Y	Y	N		4cup	Y
Cheese. Melt. Add vitamin B2 and HCl, stir well or cook twice.	N	Y	Y	N	N	4/2 oz.	Y

HEALTHY RECIPES

	has asbestos	has dye	has benzene (pesticide)	has mold	dip in HCl (2 dl/cup)	add HCl (to serving)	add B2
Eggs, wash and dry first; soak in HCl-water or Lugol's (1 drop per quart)	N	N	N	N	N	1egg	N
Half 'n half	N	Y	Y	N		4cup	Y
Milk	N	Y	Y	N		2cup	Y
Whipping cream	N	Y	Y	N		6cup	Y
Yogurt, plain	N	Y	Y	N		6cup	Y

SWEETS

	has asbestos	has dye	has benzene (pesticide)	has mold	dip in HCl (2 dl/cup)	add HCl (to serving)	add B2
Flavoring, incl. maple, vanilla, lemon.	N	Y	Y	Y	N	Y	Y
Maple syrup. Bring to a boil first.	N	N	Y	Y	N	Y	Y
Sweet baked goods	Y	Impossible to remove asbestos. Avoid.					
Sugar, incl. white, brown, confectioners, raw, fructose.	Y	Too difficult to get asbestos out. Only manufacturer's sucrose and Paraguayan organic sugar was safe.					
Honey (commercial)	Y	Too difficult to get asbestos out. Avoid.					
Honey (local), sterilize	N	N	N	N	N	Y	N

OTHER FOODS

	has asbestos	has dye	has benzene (pesticide)	has mold	dip in HCl (2 dl/cup)	add HCl (to serving)	add B2
Coffee, boil twice; then filter twice. Sterilize	Y	Use double paper filter.					
Herbal teas, boil twice.	N	Y	Y	Y	N	2cup	Y
Meat, fish, fowl. Cook regular; then microwave to sterilize, or cook twice, cool between.	N	Y	Y	N	Y	Y	Y
Olive oil, coconut oil, lard	N	Y	Y	N	N	2cup	Y
Pasta	N	N	N	Y	Y	Y	N
Spices, salt; sterilize	N	Y	Y	Y	N	Y	Y

Food Guidelines

It is impossible to remember everything about every food, but in general do not buy foods that are highly processed. Here are a few foods; see if you can guess whether they should be in your diet or not.

breads	Yes, but only from a bakery, and <u>never</u> wrapped in plastic.
toast	No. It has benzopyrene and tungsten. Yes, if made on a cookie sheet or in a frying pan.
cheese	Yes, if used in baked dishes.
chicken	Only if cooked for 20 minutes at boiling point, as in soup, or canned (never prepare raw chicken yourself).
wine with dinner	No.
peanut butter	Yes if you grind it yourself and add ¼ tsp. vitamin C powder as you grind.
cottage cheese	No, it can't be sterilized easily.
desserts	Yes, but again, only if flavored with safe extracts.
rice	Yes, if vitamin C is added before cooking. Use white only, brown is too moldy.
pasta	Yes, with homemade sauce and vitamin C.
Jell-O™	No, it has artificial flavor and color.
egg dishes	Yes, but not "imitation", cholesterol-free or cholesterol-reduced varieties.
fish, seafood	Yes!
soy foods (tofu)	No. It's the extensive processing that taints it.
soup	Yes, if seasoned only with herbs (no bouillon cube).
sugar	Yes, Turbinado or brown if treated with vitamin C.
herb tea	Yes, if not in a bag and not in a mixture of herbs.
cheesecake	Yes.

Choose brands with the shortest list of ingredients. Alternate brands every time you shop.

Daily Diet

Salt

Use <u>pure</u> salt only, like for laboratory use. Store salt could have additives and often has *Ascaris* eggs and mold.

Two to One Sodium-Potassium Salt

- **2 cups pure salt**
- **1 cup potassium chloride**

Mix. Store in tightly closed glass jar with rice added to absorb moisture. Use salt shaker without a metal lid. A one-to-one mixture is even more beneficial.

B-C Salt

Easy way to get B_2 and vitamin C into all your food.
- **½ cup pure salt or sodium-potassium salt**
- **1 capsule vitamin B2**
- **½ tsp. vitamin C (ascorbic acid) powder**

Shake together in closed jar. Pour into closeable non-metal salt shaker. When using salt in cooking, don't wait until the end to add it. It needs to be twice-cooked itself, besides raising the boiling point of the food to be cooked.

Your diet will be very low in sodium salt because in the 21 Day Program you need to consume your daily potassium gluconate first, which you "salt" your food with. This is beneficial because sick tissues become overloaded with sodium. Pulling the sodium out of them with potassium in the diet (or cesium as a medicine) helps them recover.

Milk

When cows were free and roamed in meadows of grass and flowers, they produced a moderate amount of milk, a moderate amount of manure and money and a large amount of health in growing children. Allergies and disorders were not so rampant.

But now cows are fed quite unnatural food (soybeans, yeast culture, carbohydrates) to increase milk production. These processed concentrates and even the water in their trough now give her daily doses of chlorox bleach. In fact, dairymen are encouraged to pour <u>extra</u> bleach into their water trough, and no mention is made of the NSF kind or that two kinds exist. Now cows are becoming immunodepressed, like humans, getting recurrent mastitis and necessitating lots of antibiotics. They, too, develop increased parasitism. We would expect many "Flu" attacks as a cow's body manages to kill its own flukes. Cows also get more than their share of digestion problems from their unnatural food, so that phenolic allergens would be expected. She could be expected to get prion protein attacks from so many free hypothalamus cells and not enough pepsin to digest them. Periods of dizziness, loss of appetite and staggering would result, which could explain BSE. Lowered productivity as a goal (!) for cows seems like an intelligent solution, so all these trends can be reversed while it is still possible. If we lose the milk industry to prion increase we will lose the beef industry, too. Dairy and beef producers should take a preventive approach, not adversarial.

With a heavily parasitized cow we would expect to see Bacillus cereus and tyramine in her milk. And we always do, even in cheese and all other dairy products. In fact tyramine is considered to be a headache-causer in allergy textbooks. (Nutmeg kills these bacteria.)

Switching to goat milk by sick people is another intelligent solution, to reduce allergens obtained from cow's milk.

Even goat milk provides more lactose than can be quickly digested. We use only Mexican heavy whipping cream, without lactose, and only for recovering patients. After you are well, goat milk, frozen to disinfect, then boiled 10 min. to denature allergens, would be a great help for your nutrition.

Sweeteners

All granulated forms of sugar varieties I purchased at USA grocery stores or health food stores had asbestos fibers and D-mannitol in them, not to mention chlorox.

Organic sugar from Paraguay and Mexican sugars did not have asbestos.

Sucrose purchased from a chemical supply company did not have asbestos, nor D-mannitol or other pollutants.

Honey had asbestos fibers except when locally produced. Clover honey routinely had coumarin allergen. Orange blossom honey had many allergens. All honey has fructose, normally a desirable form of sugar if not overdone. But fructose is the antigen for RBCs and should be *avoided in blood cancers, liver failure and malaria.* Honey should be tested for gold and strontium, beryllium, vanadium and chromium, air pollutants that land on flowers.

Inositol is slightly sweet but the best choice of all. It is a much needed food factor. It does not feed yeast. Used daily it makes IP6 (inositol hexa phosphate) much more efficient at uranium removal.

Maple syrup very frequently has gallic acid. Boiling one minute destroys it. Very many varieties have ASA (aspirin); test first.

Dextrose is a "powdered sugar" variety. It is usually made from corn and carries CORN antigen as well as air pollutants, strontium and beryllium. Dextrose is the sugar used in IV solutions. They should be tested for strontium, beryllium and CORN antigen.

Agave syrup often has caffeic acid and cinnamic acid, but boiling destroys both. However, it also has fructose, which yields mannitol when boiled.

Plain fruit juices can be used as sweeteners. But when yeast is a problem even plain and natural sugars should be avoided. *Always avoid in breast, skin and brain cancers.*

The land of sweets is obviously strewn with land mines. If you are living dangerously, at least minimize each one by changing the variety at every meal.

All honey, syrups or sugars should be zappicated to destroy phenolic food chemicals besides destroying asbestos, mold spores, and parasite eggs. Add vitamin C as soon as it arrives from the supermarket. Warm it first, then stir in $\frac{1}{4}$ tsp. per pint.

Water

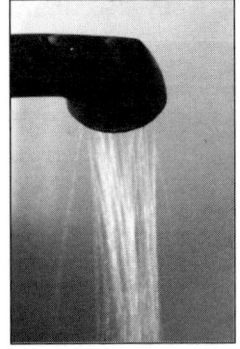

Use cold tap water only, never bottled water. The bottling process adds traces of antiseptic and solvents which include isopropyl alcohol, xylene, and toluene. Let your faucet run in the morning until one gallon has been lost. This flushes possible overnight accumulations of pipe material.

Do not use ice cubes. If you like cold water, store it in a glass container in the refrigerator, but do not drink if it is over a day old.

Do not purchase water from dispensers (again, because of sterilization contaminants). Carry your water in glass bottles. Plastic exudes plasticizers while allowing bacteria to permeate and culture in it. Do not drink out of personal dispenser bottles—they are immediately contaminated with bacteria. Sterilize your water while in foreign countries by boiling twice and later adding HCl.

Bread

According to Syncrometer® tests, homemade bread has beta-glucans, known to stimulate Natural Killer cell activity (immunity).

Make homemade bread using cake yeast. Ask your grocer to order it. Keep refrigerated. (Granulated yeast had residues of solvents and petroleum products.) All the flours on the supermarket shelves tested free of aflatoxin. Use water instead of milk for the recipes during a dairy-free period.

White bread purchased at a bakery is safe if ¼ inch is trimmed off the bottom where petroleum grease (bringing benzene) was used in the bread pan. Here, also, you would find silicone being used as a "non-stick agent."

Yeast evidently brings RAS oncogene to the human diet. Boiling and baking kills most of it, so the Syncrometer® test is negative for it, unless searched for at the chromosome sites. Full spectrum light takes over 20 minutes to kill it at the gene level. Treat all yeast or bread for 20 minutes or more! The RAS oncogene promptly multiplies and spreads in us, even if we eat it in its latent form. If you accidentally take some, take 3 doses of Frankincense.

Eggs

In earlier books I gave egg recipes, knowing they had malvin and gallic acid allergens, and knowing they had hypothalamus and pituitary cells afloat in them. I thought they could be made safe with special treatments. But since then I have found the MYC virus, the SV40 virus and sometimes even OPT itself in eggs. Not all eggs have all of these. It probably depends on the animal waste and preservatives in their feed. Free-range chickens could present a different picture. But without testing by Syncrometer®, it seems to me to be quite unwise to eat either chickens or eggs.

Eggs, even raw eggs, are safe if you pull out the white ropey cord with a fork (this is the location of tissue bits of pituitary and hypothalamus), add 3 HCl drops per egg and zap or zappicate the rest. But eggs have more problems: **malvin**, which causes seizures, and **gallic acid**, which triggers the SV 40 virus and inflames the pancreas. You can destroy these, too, if you zappicate 10 minutes or more.

When feeding a sick pet, a raw egg daily does wonders, while any number of <u>cooked</u> eggs does much less. Now that you know how to eat raw eggs safely, it would be great nutrition for you to eat one daily for two weeks! Be sure to add the HCl while stirring. It, too, "denatures" and destroys the live tissue bits. Drink only one daily of these super nutrition recipes to avoid becoming allergic to them. Some of the following recipes use eggs; use your own discretion.

Beans, Dried Peas, Lentils & Rice

These foods have hard centers even after regular cooking. *Shigella* bacteria and *Ascaris* eggs not only survive there, they are helped to multiply. The eggs hatch into larvae on a massive scale during the cooling down period, ready to invade. But once hatched, they are vulnerable and  can be killed by boiling briefly again or light treatment. Refried beans or rice and twice cooked peas and lentils are safe. Pressure cooking these foods until very soft speeds up the process, but still does not kill everything at first. After a 10 minute cool-down (adding cold water shortens this to 5 minutes), bring to boil again for 5 minutes. They must still be sterilized at time of serving.

Meats

A big advantage has been gained from electrical treatments. All parasite eggs and stages can be killed quickly and to any depth, by any one of the three methods. You can now cook, bake, poach, or fry them the usual way. Do not grill.

Fruits & Vegetables

Most are sprayed with combinations of wax, dye, pesticide, anti-sprouter, anti-mold, etc. Fast green (Food Green 3) is present on most and brings with it the lanthanide elements. This dye, plus lanthanides are water-soluble and penetrate the food deeply. But double soaking in hot water for 1 minute removes it. Even organic bananas, pears, grapefruit, and potatoes must be double soaked this way.

Peel all vegetables and fruit that <u>can</u> be peeled. It is true that the peel contains beneficial nutrients and roughage. But safety is more important. And since you are now returning to an "all natural" diet, your nutrition will already be much better. Peeling lets you see fungus (mold) invasion that is otherwise invisible. The mold in potatoes produces zearalenone. Stick to red and white varieties that have far less mold.

Remember, kill fertilize parasites by soaking all greens and unpeeled vegetables in Lugol's solution for one minute to kill Ascaris and tapeworm eggs. They may be present from the manure used for fertilizer and they don't wash off!

Complete Meal Drinks

When a meal is missed weight is lost and the body is stressed. During dental work, especially, weight is easily lost that cannot be regained. Every effort should be made to keep up the usual calorie intake. You can make a drinkable "meal" that needs no preparation, and provides the fat, protein, and carbohydrate essential for life. The principles are:

- ½ cup heavy whipping cream
- ½ cup water or barley water
- 1 tbsp. safe sweetener
- 5 capsules mixed amino acids
- NO vegetable oil to avoid triggering oncoviruses
- NO eggs or milk

(Read label for phenylalanine or tryptophane presence in case you must avoid these). This is the protein source.

Variations: ½ capsule nutmeg, 1 tsp. clove tea, 1 tsp. hydrangea tea, or any other spice, ground nuts.

Stir all together. The whipping cream should already have been treated (overnight) with ¼ capsule lactase per pint, then ozonated. Take lipase-containing digestive enzymes with this. Change the spice at each meal.

CALORIES: 477

HEALTHY RECIPES

EZ Meal
- 1 egg
- 1 tbsp. oil, safe variety
- 1 tbsp. honey
- ¼ tsp. nutmeg (freshly ground)
- sodium-potassium salt (to taste)
- water to make 1 cup total

CALORIES = 255

EZ Dairy Meal
- 1 egg
- 1 tbsp. oil, safe variety
- 1 tbsp. honey
- ¼ tsp. nutmeg (freshly ground)
- sodium-potassium salt (to taste)
- goat milk to make 1 cup

CALORIES = 345

Mini Flax Oil EZ Meal
- 1 egg
- 1 tsp. flaxseed oil
- 1 tbsp. honey
- ¼ tsp. nutmeg (freshly ground)
- ¼ tsp. cloves
- ½ cup coconut milk

CALORIES = 210

Flax Oil EZ Meal
- 1 egg
- 1 tsp. flaxseed oil
- 2 tsp. oil, safe variety
- ½ cup coconut whipping cream (100 ml = 250 calories)
- 1 tbsp. honey
- ¼ tsp. nutmeg (freshly ground)
- water to make 1 cup (optional)

CALORIES = 550

Remove stringy part of egg white. Add 3 drops HCl (5%), mixing thoroughly with plastic fork or blender. Add remaining ingredients and blend or mix with a plastic fork. Zappicate for 10 minutes.

For a change of flavor add cardamom, coriander, licorice powder, ½ tsp. grated lemon peel, but keep the nutmeg. Also try Agave syrup, different kinds of honey or Mexican sugar.

A sick person needs 2000 calories a day to recover.

The basic recipe combines a protein (egg), a natural fat (cream, oil) and natural carbohydrate (honey, syrup). You may design your own variations.

Blender Meals
(to prevent weight loss)

You won't lose weight during dental work with these recipes, even if you don't know what you're drinking. For emaciated patients, add 1 Tbsp. safe butter to each recipe.

Blended Turkey

- **cooked rice, 1 serving**
- **cooked turkey, 1 serving**
- **water, about 1 cup**
- **avocado, ripe but without mold spots inside**

Place rice, turkey, water, salt in blender and blend 4 seconds at a time till drinkable. Add chunks of avocado later, to provide something solid.

Blended Stew

- any cooked meat or fish dish
- any vegetable dish
- anything raw and green or yellow
- water, about 1 cup
- pure salt
- an herb, like oregano leaf, thyme leaf, cilantro, disinfected

Put a serving of each in the blender along with water, salt to suit taste and herbs. Blend 4 seconds at a time, adding more water till drinkable.

Variations: Use less water to keep it thick and spoonable. Adjust salt to needs.

Beverages

Quick Vanilla Drink

- 1 tbs. coconut oil
- 1 egg
- 1 tbs. sweetening
- ¼ tsp. vanilla
- pinch of vitamin B2 potassium salt to taste
- water to make 1 cup total

Quick Almond Drink

Same ingredients as above, except add almond milk.

Four Egg Nogs

Remove the white ropey part of egg. Blend each recipe. Add 3 drops HCl to each. The nutmeg destroys tyramine and *Bacillus cereus* bacteria in the dairy product and in you!

- 1 raw egg
- 1 cup goat milk
- 1 tbsp. honey
- ¼ tsp. nutmeg powder (freshly ground)

Cream Shake

- $^1/_2$ cup heavy whipping cream (from a health food store)
- 1 raw egg
- 1 tbsp. honey
- ¼ tsp. nutmeg

Coconut Egg Nog

- 1 raw egg
- 1 cup coconut "milk"
- ¼ tsp. nutmeg powder
- 1 tbsp. Agave syrup

Egg Nog Cream Shake

- 1 egg yolk
- 1 cup half & half, organic
- ¼ tsp. nutmeg
- 1 tbsp. honey

Hot Vanilla Milk

Add one inch of vanilla bean and one tsp. honey to a glass of milk and bring to a near boil. You may add a pinch of cinnamon or other pure spice. You may use vanilla extract.

Lemon / Oil Drink

Soak one lemon twice in hot water, drying each time; peel thinly; blend it whole, rind, seeds and all. Strain and discard pulp. Add 1 tbs. olive oil and enough honey and water (1½ cup) to make it tasty. Read the label on the lemon-packaging; avoid those that have been sprayed. Ask your grocer if that information is not obvious. Sterilize with 2 drops HCl.

Whole Lemonade

- **1 whole lemon**
- **3 tbsp. honey**
- **1 cup water (with 1 drop HCl)**

Double hot wash the lemon, cut away flower and stem ends, cut in pieces and place in blender, seeds, peel and all. Add honey and water. Blend. Strain through a course plastic strainer. Freeze the pulp for future use. This recipe removes asbestos, aluminum and mercury from your body tissues. The effect can be very pronounced if you have already stopped getting these pollutants into yourself. Do not consume more than one lemon a day to prevent becoming allergic to it. In fact, do not consume more than one citrus fruit in a day.

This beverage is the perfect hiding place for even the worst of supplements. The hydrangea powder, even cysteine, thioctic acid, glutathione, and taurine can be hidden when ½ tsp. nutmeg and 4 tbsp. honey are used in the recipe.

Digestive enzymes, betaine, and even wormwood will be hidden when ¼ tsp. cloves are added.

Lemonade

1 cup fresh lemon juice, 1 cup honey, 1½ quarts water. Bring honey and water to a boil if you plan to keep it several days. Then add lemon juice and store in the refrigerator.

Watermelon / Banana

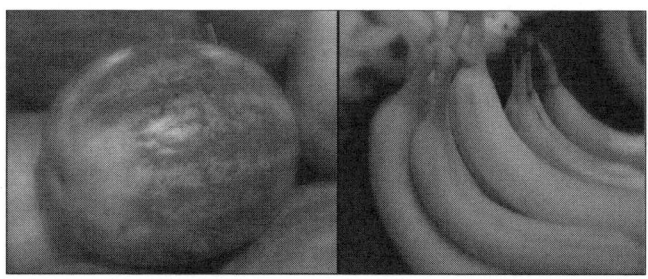

- **One watermelon**
- **6 to 8 bananas (soaked twice in hot water for 1 minute and dried before peeling)**

Peel the watermelon so thickly that only the juicy red part is used. Discard all seeds. Blend and refrigerate. To serve, put one cup in blender with ½ banana. Add 2 drops HCl per cup when served.

Melon / Lemon

- **1 honeydew melon (peeled and cleaned)**
- **1 peeled lemon (wash twice with hot water first)**
- **sweetening**

Blend or juice. Add 2 drops HCl per cup.
Variation: use 2 lemons and call it "lemon/melon."

Fresh Pineapple Juice

Peel a pineapple. Remove all soft spots. Cut it into cubes. Extract the juice by putting the pineapple through a food

grinder or a blender. There will be very little pulp. Strain the juice and serve it on ice with sprigs of mint. Makes about 1½ cups of juice. Mix the pulp with an equal amount of clover honey and use as topping (keep in freezer) for homemade ice cream (below), pancakes, or yogurt.

Honeydew Ambrosia

- **One honeydew melon**

Peel honeydew so thickly that only the sweet flesh is used. Discard all seeds. Liquefy in blender or put through juicer. Sterilize with HCl when serving.

Variation: Add almond milk in equal parts.

Fresh Tomato Juice

Simmer for ½ hour:

- **12 medium-sized raw, ripe tomatoes**
- **½ cup water**
- **2 ribs celery with leaves**
- **½ bay leaf**
- **3 sprigs parsley**

Strain these ingredients. Season with: 1 tsp. salt (aluminum-free), ¼ tsp. paprika, ½ tsp. honey. Serve thoroughly chilled. Makes about 4 servings.

Almond Milk

- **1 cup almonds with brown skins on**
- **Potassium gluconate or sodium-potassium salt**

Soak almonds for two days in water, changing the water several times. This loosens the skin. Or pour boiling water over them and let cool. Slip skins off by hand. Blend, by adding water to drinkable consistency. Add $1/8$ tsp. salt per pint. Sterilize with 4 drops of HCl per cup.

Variations: add vitamin C and sweetening to taste; add half and half when dairy is allowed. This is very nutritious; helps gain weight.

Coconut Milk

- **meat from one coconut (carefully washed and brown skin removed)**
- **3 cups water**

Place chunks in blender to liquefy. Strain. Save pulp for toppings and desserts. Add sweetening to taste and 2 drops HCl per cup when serving to kill bacteria from handling.

Variation: add pineapple juice in equal amounts; add 1 egg, 1 tbs. sweetening, $1/16$ tsp. salt per cup to make another "feed"; add ½ banana to 1 cup liquid and blend.

Coconut - Tangerine Juice

- **milk of one fresh coconut (give the meat away)**
- **2 tangerines**

At a certain time of year the new coconut crop is in. The meat is soft and the "milk" plentiful. If someone would crack and clean it for you, you could consume one a week. Until you are well you must have the "milk" only; the "meat" has too much plant oil for your digestion. Nevertheless, you will be getting both organic germanium and selenium. Peel the tangerines after 2 hot washes. Save the peels in the freezer for future flavoring. Pour the milk into a blender. Add the tangerines, seeds and all. Blend 4 seconds only. Immediately strain through steel strainer. Do not store this; drink immediately. *Optional:* To make a slurpee out of this, add a piece of frozen banana before blending.

Coconut Smoothie

- **²/₃ cup shredded or flaked, sweetened coconut from a package**
- **½ cup water (plus 1 drop HCl)**

Zappicate the entire package. Then blend coconut and water until smooth; spoon onto cereal, desserts or homemade bread. Add more water or use more powerful blender for a drinkable beverage. This, too, will "cover" any unpalatable supplement when nutmeg or cloves are added as spices. Note: All brands of packaged coconut tested Negative for common pollutants.

Red Milk

- **1 small raw red beet (peeled)**
- **1 cup goat milk**
- **1 Fenu-Thyme capsule**

Blend the beet until drinkable or strain and use juice. Add milk and spice (plus 3 drops of HCl); then blend again.

Variations: 1 turmeric capsule instead of Fenu-Thyme; use coconut milk instead of goat milk. Raw beet juice can destroy many food phenolic chemicals, including phenol itself. Taken as a relish or juice with meals, it is a great help to the liver. Maybe that is why it is known as a liver tonic. Red beets can raise the red blood cell count, too. Nevertheless, do not overdo the amount of raw beet. A moderate amount is 1 tbsp. per meal.

Maple Milk Shake

For each milk shake, blend or shake together: 1 glass of milk and 2 tablespoons maple syrup.

Yankee Drink

Mix together 1 gal. water, 3 cups honey, ½ cup fresh lemon juice or distilled white vinegar, and 1 tsp. ginger.

C-Milk

Milk can absorb a surprising amount of vitamin C powder without curdling or changing its flavor. Try ½ tsp. in a glass of cold milk. Add nutmeg for a flavor change.

Half and Half

Mix equal parts whipping cream and milk or water. Boil and chill.

Cream Shake

Blend one egg yolk, one cup of half and half, honey to sweeten and cinnamon or nutmeg. Drink only once a day.

Raw Certified Milk

Find this at your health food store. Raw milk has a special factor, lactoferrin, missing from the liver, spleen and bone marrow in cases of anemia and cancer. One glass of raw milk replenishes for over a week! Boiling for 10 seconds does not destroy it! Add a pinch of salt before boiling. It is not present in ordinary pasteurized milk.

Baby Coconut Juice

At a certain time of year the new coconut crop is in. The "meat" is soft and the "milk" plentiful. If you are lucky enough to be near a coconut bar where someone cracks and cleans them for you, eat two or three a week. They are full of germanium and selenium in organic form.

Blend the meat with the milk or with another juice variety. Drink the milk plain or made into eggnog. Add 1 drop hydrochloric acid to sanitize.

Coconut - Tangerine Juice

(organic germanium and selenium)

- **one fresh coconut (keep the meat in freezer)**
- **2 tangerines (hot washed)**
- **milk of coconut**

At a certain time of year the new coconut crop is in. The meat is soft and the "milk" plentiful. If someone would crack and clean it for you, you could consume one a week. Until you are no longer coughing, avoid coconut, though, because the natural oil somehow increases viruses. But after lungs improve you can get both organic germanium and selenium this delicious way. Pour the milk and a piece of "meat" into a blender. Add the whole tangerines, seeds and all. Blend 4 seconds only. Immediately strain through steel strainer. Do not store this; drink immediately.

Buttermilk - C I

Stir 1 tsp. vitamin C powder into a glass of milk. Add a pinch of potassium chloride. Additional seasoning may be pepper and herbs. Stir and enjoy.

Buttermilk - C II

Mix equal amounts of heavy whipping cream and ultra pasteurized goat milk. Stir in 1½ tsp. vitamin C powder per 8 oz. glass. Add $1/8$ capsule of nutmeg powder. If it does not form flakes readily, add ¼ tsp. citric acid per glass. **Citric acid kills Salmonella bacteria.**

Green Dinosaur

- one beet leaf, or one handful of watercress or spinach
- ½ grapefruit or 1 pear, peach, nectarine
- ½ pineapple, several apricots or other fruit, including the seeds (choose one variety only); it should be completely ripe or cooked.
- 1 tbsp. honey

Don't use a rhubarb leaf or a non-edible! Beet leaves contain a lot of oxalic acid. One leaf is enough. Change variety often. Don't purchase greens at a health food store or any grocery where spraying is done on the display shelves. Give each item two hot washes although it will certainly wilt the greens, but it doesn't matter when making a drink.

Blend greens to make ¼ cup. Peel fruit. Add fruit and honey; blend again. Zappicate. Strain and save the pulp, or add enough water (plus HCl) to make it drinkable.

This beverage can draw <u>aluminum</u>, <u>mercury</u>, <u>asbestos</u> and <u>copper</u> out of the body in large amounts and into the urine. Drink a different one every day.

Green Goodness

- head lettuce
- grapefruit

Other varieties of lettuce, as well as parsley and spinach, tested *Positive* for benzene. This was also the case for health food store greens, no doubt due to the new practice of spraying for "freshness." If in doubt ozonate the greens for 20 minutes; then rinse in water with baking soda added. Blend lettuce in juicer or blender to make ¼ cup. Add grapefruit and blend again to make 1 cup. Strain.

Green Drink

- **cabbage, kale, Swiss chard, turnip greens, or any other broad-leafed edible tops**
- **grapefruit, lemon, apple, pear, pineapple (strawberries and grapes are too moldy to risk)**

Don't use rhubarb or nonedibles! Swiss chard and beet leaves contain a lot of oxalic acid. One leaf of each is enough.

Blend greens to make ¼ cup. Add fruit to make a total of one cup. Blend together. Strain.

Barley Water

This is an ancient "medicine". It has organic manganese.

- **whole barley, frozen or ozonated to sterilize**

Test for bromine first; do not eat brominated grains. It cannot be removed. It sequesters polonium in you.

Add four times as much water as barley and let stand at least four hours. Then refrigerate. Decant and drink. Cooking changes some of it to plain manganese metal that feeds Shigella. Don't cook it if not necessary. It can be made into chewy, spicy, uncooked breakfast cereal. Vinegar kills Shigella, but can't be used in colon or prostate cancer.

Variation: Any kind of safe rice can be made into a medicinal "rice water" that provides calories and B vitamins.

My Own Soda Pop

This is excellent for stomach distress. Put 1 tsp. citric acid, 2 tbs. vegetable glycerin, 2 tbs. honey, and 1 lemon, juiced by hand, into a quart jar and fill with cold water. Refrigerate until ready to use. Then add 1 tsp. baking soda (chemically pure only), and shake, keeping the lid tight. Pour over a few ice cubes. Many variations are possible: other fruit concentrates, make in the blender, can be used along with some lemon juice;

for example, 2 blended whole apples (peeled), and blended pineapple, orange or grapefruit. Always add a bit of lemon to give it zip. You may add a pinch of ginger or other spice.

Note: The amount of sodium in ½ tsp. baking soda is .476 grams. If you have heart disease, high blood pressure, or edema, use potassium bicarbonate instead. Ask your doctor what an acceptable amount of sodium or potassium bicarbonate is. I would suggest limiting yourself to one glass of soda pop a day, even if you do not have heart disease.

Another Note: the citric acid kills bacteria, while the carbonation brings relief.

My Own Super C-Pop

This is an excellent way to get lots of vitamin C into a child and relieve stomach distress at the same time. Squeeze 1 slice of lemon and 1 whole orange into an 8 ounce bottle that has a tight lid. Add 1 tsp. vitamin C powder (ascorbic acid), ¼ tsp. citric acid, and 2 tbs. vegetable glycerin (you may also experiment with honey for sweetness). Fill the bottle to the top with cold water. Then add ½ tsp. chemically pure baking soda and close tightly. Shake briefly and serve immediately.

Zoom Juice

This beverage can give you too much energy. Drink during daytime.
- **1 tbsp. molasses (organic)**
- **1 tbsp. chlorophyll**
- **1 tbsp. pomegranate juice or paste**

Stir all into a tall glass of water. Add three drops HCl. Zappicate ingredients or the final product. *Variations*: Add coconut milk or goat milk instead of water. Add a pinch of citric acid. Add 1/8 tsp. watercress powder. Many supplements can be hidden in this beverage. Pomegranate removes dyes from liver. Watercress powder destroys dyes even in your glass.

Mini - Zoom Juice

- 1 tsp. molasses
- 1 tsp. chlorophyll
- 1 tsp. pomegranate juice or paste

Stir into one cup water (plus 1 drop HCl). Drink hot or cold.

Nopales Drink

- 1 small leaf pad of Nopales (prickly pear cactus), sanitized with 1 drop HCl smeared with your finger
- 1 tsp. pomegranate paste or 1 cup pomegranate juice
- 1 tsp. molasses
- 1 tsp. nutmeg powder
- 3 drops HCl

Blend till smooth. Add more liquid till drinkable.

Spreads

Nearly Butter

- **10 oz. coconut oil**
- **2 oz. olive oil**
- **½ capsule riboflavin (vitamin B₂)**
- **⅛ teaspoon pure salt or sodium-potassium salt**

If coconut oil is solidified, melt it first by warming. Then add oils together in jar. Most oil contains *Ascaris* eggs and must be sterilized. Add HCl drops, 2 per cup. Shake until uniformly mixed. Add riboflavin and salt. Shake again. Pour into mold or butter dish. Refrigerate. Remove from mold with hot water.

Note about colors: coenzyme Q10 gives a butter-yellow color. Riboflavin gives lemon-yellow color. Turmeric is another safe yellow colorant. You may use these other colorants as long as a pinch of B_2 is added to detoxify any benzene.

Butter

Although it comes from cow's milk, it does not have the tissue bits of pituitary and hypothalamus glands that the milk itself and cheeses have. Unfortunately, most butter is spiced— even when labeled organic. The spice includes "onion", favorite food of Fasciolopsis. But boiling destroys it, so I recommend boiling and, later, zappicating to destroy traces of dyes.

Real Butter

- 1 pint whipping cream
- ¼ tsp. watercress powder or freshly made watercress juice
- 8 drops HCl

Put all ingredients into a plastic container or a glass jar with enough empty space left to shake well.

Shake for 5 minutes. Soon the cream feels "thick". It gets thicker and thicker until suddenly it all separates into butter and buttermilk. Keep shaking till a solid ball of butter is formed. Pour off the buttermilk. Don't consume this. Throw it out. It contains the dyes, asbestos and heavy metals that may have been in the cream.

Wash the butter pellet with 4 changes of very cold water or until the water remains clear. Finally, sculpt and display your butter on a serving plate or mash it into a regular butter dish. Zappicate and refrigerate. Makes about ¼ pound.

Coconut Butter

- 10 oz. coconut oil
- 2 oz. olive oil
- ½ capsule riboflavin (vitamin B2)
- ⅛ tsp. pure salt or sodium-potassium salt (to taste)

If coconut oil is solidified, melt it first by warming. Then add oils together in jar. Shake the two oils until uniformly mixed.

Add riboflavin and salt. Shake again. Pour into mold or butter dish. Refrigerate. Remove from mold with hot water.

Note about colors: coenzyme Q10 gives a butter-yellow color. Riboflavin gives lemon-yellow color. Turmeric is another safe yellow colorant. Zappicate all.

Spreadable Butter

Bring one-quarter pound of butter to a boil in a saucepan. Add a pinch of salt. Count to ten, while it bubbles. Add a pinch of vitamin C. Then add olive oil in equal amount or to suit. Reheat and pour into a butter bowl. Do not save any liquid that separates at the bottom. Refrigerate.

Peanut Butter

Use fresh unsalted roasted peanuts—they will be white on the first day they arrive at the health food store from the distributor. Or shell fresh roasted peanuts yourself, throwing away all shriveled or darkened nuts. Grind, adding salt and vitamin C (¼ tsp. per pint) as you go. Take your own salt shaker with built in vitamin C to the health food store where you grind it. For spreadability, especially for children, mix an equal volume of cold butter, previously boiled, to freshly ground peanut butter. This improves spreadability and digestibility of the hard nut particles. This will probably be the most heavenly peanut butter your mouth has ever experienced.

Preserves

Keep 3 or 4 kinds on hand, such as peach, pineapple, and pear. Peel and chop the fruit. It should not have any bruises. If you use a metal knife, rinse the fruit lightly afterwards. Add just enough water to keep the fruit from sticking as it is cooked (usually a few tablespoons). Then add an equal amount of honey, or to taste and heat again to boiling. Put in sterile jars in refrigerator. Make lemon marmalade the same way, slicing the fruit and peeling thinly. Be sure the lemons were not sprayed! Always add vitamin C powder to a partly used jar to inhibit mold. Never use up partly molded fruit by making preserves out of it. Never use "soft" (actually moldy) bananas to make banana bread. Never make guacamole out of soft (actually moldy) avocados. Throw them out.

Most preserves are easily made in minutes.

- **1 cup fruit**
- **1 tbs. water**
- **sweetening**

Soak twice for 1 minute each time in very hot water and dry; this removes wax-spray, dye and asbestos. Peel. Heat to boiling in water, stirring with wooden spoon. When done, add half as much sweetening as fruit and bring to boil again. Add HCl drops at point of use (2 drops per cup) and light-treat.

Variations: add lemon juice for extra zip.

Marmalade

- **2½ cups water**
- **2½ quarts whole ranges**
- **2 whole grapefruits**
- **1 lemon**
- **5 to 6 cups (according to your taste) safe granulated sugar**
- **½ tsp. vitamin C**

Boil water. Add oranges, grapefruits and lemon that have been double hot-washed, and put through a food processor until coarsely chopped. Bring to a boil; then cook on low heat, uncovered, about 35 minutes. Stir with wooden spoon occasionally and pick out any seeds that rise to the surface. Stir in sugar, again bringing to a boil. Simmer an additional 20 minutes. Stir in vitamin C. Ladle into sterilized glass jars. Cover with plastic lids. Zappicate each jar when cool.

There are many uses for marmalade besides being good on homemade bread and butter. Try on homemade ice cream.

Kumquat Marmalade

If you feel starved for "orange" flavor, you will love this recipe.
- **2½ cups water**
- **2½ quarts whole kumquats, stems removed**
- **2 whole grapefruits**
- **1 lemon**
- **5 or 6 cups powdered sugar**
- **½ tsp. vitamin C**

Wash the kumquats, grapefruits, lemon, and put through a food processor until coarsely chopped. Bring the water to a boil, add the fruit, and bring to a boil again. Then cook on low heat, uncovered, about 35 minutes. Stir with wooden spoon occasionally and pick out any seeds that rise to the surface. Stir in sugar according to your taste, again bringing to a boil. Simmer an additional 20 minutes. Stir in vitamin C. Ladle into sterilized glass jars. Cover with plastic lids.

There are many uses for marmalade besides being good with bread and butter. Try adding to cooked, mashed yams, on homemade ice cream, etc.

Pancakes

Maria's Best Pancakes

- **32 ounces of Bob's Red Mill rice flour**
- **1 stick of butter**
- **²/₃ to ¾ cup of heavy cream**
- **24½ oz. water (depending on consistency)**
- **raisins or currents (Fairfield, Sun Maid)**
- **1 Tbsp. baking soda**
- **1 tsp. salt**
- **½ Tbsp. vitamin C**
- **2 eggs**

Disinfect all ingredients. Combine all, except water, in large bowl. Mix together then add water slowly to desired consistency. Fry in butter.

Cereals

Barley is the best choice. Other cereal grains should be nitrogen packed to avoid developing menadione. Store in freezer after opening; do not ozonate to avoid oxidation.

Choose only the coarse varieties, not finely ground, or very thin flakes.

Corn is a poor choice because it picks up air pollutants.

Rice is second best, with least antigens.

Three Granolas

Granola I

- 7 cups rolled oats
- 1 tsp. salt (pure variety)
- 1 cup wheat germ (fresh, not defatted)
- ½ cup honey
- ½ cup sunflower seeds (immaculate quality)
- ½ cup milk (with pinch of vitamin C added)
- ½ cup melted butter (already boiled with vitamin C added)
- 1 cup raisins (rinsed in vitamin C water)

Mix dry ingredients together. Mix liquid ingredients and add gradually, while tossing until thoroughly mixed. Place in large ungreased pans and bake in slow (250°) oven. Stir occasionally, baking until brown and dry, usually 1-2 hours. Store in airtight container in freezer.

Granola II

- **6 cups rolled oats**
- **½ cup raw wheat germ**
- **1 cup sesame seeds**
- **1 cup sunflower seeds (raw, unsalted)**
- **1 tsp. cinnamon**
- **½ cup melted butter**
- **½ cup honey**

Preheat oven to 250°. Toss all ingredients in mixing bowl. Spread thinly on a baking sheet and bake 20-25 minutes. Stir often in order to brown evenly. When golden, remove and let cool. Makes 12 cups.

If you would like to add nuts to your granola recipes, rinse them in cold tap water first, to which vitamin C powder has been added (¼ tsp. per pint). Rub off the skins. This removes aflatoxins and malonate.

Granola III (stove top or dry roast)

It is cooked quickly right on top of the stove. The quick, sautéing gives a deep-roasted flavor to the ingredients. The brown sugar melts just a bit, slightly coating each flake.

- **2 cups raw rolled oats**
- **⅓ cup or more wheat germ**
- **⅓ cup or more sesame seeds**
- **⅓ cup or more sunflower seeds**
- **⅓ cup or more shredded coconut**
- **¼ cup brown sugar (packed and treated with vitamin C**
- **¼ tsp. salt (heaping)**

Use a large, heavy skillet. Place the oats in the skillet, turn on the heat to medium-low, and stir them constantly for 5 minutes, as they begin to roast.

Healthy Recipes

Add wheat germ, sesame seeds, sunflower seeds, and coconut. Keep both the heat and the stirring action constant for ten or more minutes.

Sprinkle in brown sugar and salt. Cook for 2-5 more minutes, still stirring. Remove from heat, cool, and store in an airtight container.

Note: this yields about 3½ cups. You can double the amounts, but it is recommended that you make smaller batches more frequently instead, for greater freshness.

Jump Start Cereal

- ¼ cup wheat germ
- ⅛ cup pomegranate paste or molasses

Zappicate all items first. Add goat milk, coconut milk or plain water to your serving.

Dressings

C-Dressing

- ½ cup safe oil
- ¼ cup fresh lemon juice
- 1 tsp. thyme, fenugreek or both (capsules are freshest, combination is Fenu-Thyme. Use 2 capsules.)
- 1 tsp. vitamin C powder
- ½ tsp. honey

Combine ingredients in a well-rinsed salad dressing bottle. Shake. Zappicate. Refrigerate. The basic recipe is the oil and lemon juice in a 2:1 ratio. After mixing these, add any pure spice desired.

This dressing is especially good in wintertime to protect you from colds. As little as 1 capsule a day of Fenu-Thyme alone, is quite effective, too. Or add home made cottage cheese for a creamy texture.

Mom's Mayo

- ¾ cup olive oil or other safe oil
- 1 egg (zappicated and 3 drops HCl added)
- ¾ tsp. salt (pure sodium chloride or sodium-potassium mixture)
- 1 tsp. sugar (safe variety)
- juice from 1 small lemon

Put egg, lemon juice, salt and sugar in blender. Begin blending. Add the oil slowly, while blending, so you can make your favorite consistency. Makes 1 cup.

Sour Cream-C

- **2 cups heavy whipping cream (cow, goat or coconut)**
- **¼ tsp. citric acid**
- **¼ tsp. vitamin C powder**
- **pinch of pure salt**

Stir until smooth. Zappicate; then refrigerate two hours before serving.

Beet Popsicles

- **red beets, peeled and cubed**

Freeze some raw beet in small plastic relish containers with lids. Cook the rest and freeze these, too. Serve one portion with each meal.

Variations: serve with a tbsp. homemade horseradish sauce; use a sour cream recipe or Mom's Mayo to mix with fresh grated horseradish for the sauce.

Queen of Hearts Dressing (hides all supplements)

Fruit juices are easily made into dressings for many purposes, over vegetables, over rice, and even over a pile of vitamins dumped from their capsules. *Avoid fruit juice in brain cancer.*

- **1 cup fruit juice**
- **½ tsp. citric acid powder (or more)**
- **1 Tbsp. sweetening**
- **2 Tbsp. thickener (rose hips, hydrangea powder, vitamins)**
- **extra spice (thyme, turmeric, fennel, nutmeg, cardamom, coriander, ginger); choose to suit the meal**

Boil fruit juice. Add to thickener slowly, while stirring to make a paste first. Add sweetening, spice, and citric acid.

The thickener can be any assortment of dry supplements that needs to "go down" at that meal. By keeping the fruit juice and citric acid mixture always handy and varied, any pile of vitamin powders can be consumed the easy way: on top of a lettuce salad. Rotate spices.

Sauces

Tomato Sauce I

Use garden grown tomatoes that have not been sprayed. Only your own garden can be trusted. You will not need the double hot wash. But you do need to zappicate for food phenolics and plain bacteria.

Peel and bring to a boil with just enough water added to keep it liquid. Use non-metal utensils. Add pure salt.

Tomato Sauce II

Choose perfect cherry or Roma tomatoes because they do not produce malvin and are often unsprayed. Test for malonic acid, though. Sterilize with Lugol's water or ozonation or freezing.
- **2 cups whole tomatoes**
- **½ cup water ¼ tsp. sodium chloride (pure) salt**
- **1 tsp. oregano or thyme leaves, organic, or fresh**

Purchased oregano needs testing for thallium besides chlorox. Bring all ingredients to a hard boil for 2 or 3 minutes in a stainless steel saucepan. Empty this into a polyethylene container as soon as cool enough. Keep refrigerated or frozen. Keep oregano frozen, too. You can use a manual "food mill" to separate peels, seeds, etc. Eat the peel if there is no danger of sprays.

Variations: Use fresh basil, if unsprayed, as seasoning.

Pasta Pizza Sauce or Red Sauce

Here are two sauces that are excellent on pasta, pizza or salads.
- **3 red peppers (chopped or in chunks)**
- **¼ cup white distilled vinegar**
- **1 small onion**
- **3 tbs. olive oil**
- **salt to taste**
- **1 cup water**

Sauce No. I

Sauté peppers and onion in olive oil for a few minutes. Add generous sprinkling of salt and a cup of water and bring to a boil. Cover pan, lower burner heat and cook for three to five more minutes. Mash (or put into blender) and add vinegar. Blend for a few seconds and add salt (if by taste more is needed). May be kept up to a month in refrigerator if stored in a glass jar with plastic or wooden lid.

Sauce No. II

Same as Sauce No. 1 except that when a sprinkling of salt is put into pan also add a ½ capsule each of Cloves, fenuthyme, and turmeric.

Cheese Sauce

Add milk to cheese in equal amounts. Gradually heat to boiling while stirring. Add more of either to obtain the desired consistency. Boil 10 seconds. Use immediatcly.

Yogurt & Cottage Cheese

Buy a yogurt maker. Be sure to use boiled milk and add vitamin C. When done add fresh blueberries, strawberries, or peaches. Use plain yogurt as starter.

Cottage Cheese "Paneer"

This tastes much better than regular cottage cheese. It's more easily digested, too. Don't throw away the liquid that remains (whey) since it has all the calcium of the milk in it. Drink ice cold on a hot day.

- **⅛ tsp. salt**
- **½ gallon milk**
- **juice of 2 lemons**

Put milk and salt in saucepan or wok and bring to boil for 10 seconds. Add juice of 1 lemon for each quart of milk. Stir and allow to boil for another few seconds. When curdled, strain through thin cloth (cheesecloth or thin dishtowel) and squeeze all liquid out until desired consistency. Should be very dry if it is to be cut into squares for vegetable dishes, but not too dry if to be used like cottage or cream cheese. Makes 1 cup.

Cottage Cheese "Zuppe"

Drop cottage cheese into a saucepan and cover with milk or cream. Add 1/8 tsp. baking soda, salt, pepper, garlic and any other herbs. Stir and boil for 20 seconds. When cool, add vitamin C (1/8 tsp. per pint).

Fast Food Cottage Cheese

Zappicate a carton of cottage cheese for 10 minutes. Zappicate the honey dispenser and heat till flowing. Add ¼ tsp. nutmeg and 10 drops HCl to the cottage cheese, stirring it in and leaving a hole in the middle. Pour in honey. For a change, add ¼ tsp. grated lemon peel, too, or the pulp from a whole lemon or other strained beverage.

Goat Cheese

If you were a cheese lover, you would enjoy getting it back on your menu by making it yourself. Make cottage cheese from 2 quarts of goat milk according to an old recipe. But add a tsp. of regular Blue Cheese before it all turns into curds. You can get addicted to this, so restrict yourself to alternate days. Add 3 drops HCl per cup to final product and zappicate.

Flax Seed

- **whole flax seed or linseed**

Throw away damaged seeds. Rinse 1 tbs. flax seed in HCl-water and drain. Set to soak in fresh HCl-water for 10 minutes or till soft enough to chew. Add to cereal, salad or later, to cottage cheese.

Soups

All home made soups are nutritious and safe, provided you use no processed ingredients (like a bouillon cube), or make them in metal pots. Use herbs and pure salt to season. The salt should be added during boiling, not at the end, to raise the boiling temperature and kill more bacteria. Always add a dash of vitamin C or vinegar to draw out calcium from soup bones for you to absorb. Soups are great for the finicky appetite.

Chicken Broth

- **One whole chicken**
- **½ white onion (peeled apart and soaked in B_2-water)**
- **1 bay leaf**
- **5 peppercorns**
- **¼ tsp. pure salt per quart water**

Cover chicken with water. When coming to a boil, skim off foam repeatedly. Then add other ingredients. Cook about 2 hours adding water to keep the level up, or pressure cook 30 minutes. Pour off the broth. Do not throw away the fat. Pack it into a "butter tub" for use in frying.

The chicken itself makes a meal, but is not yet safe for a cancer patient. It may be cooked a second time, waiting ½ hour to cool first, or microwaved, preferably in a cooking bag to retain moisture and flavor. Meat should fall apart when done. Finally, add HCl before serving. Turkey and Cornish hen can be similarly prepared.

Healthy Recipes

Cheese Soup

- 4 cups home made chicken broth
- ¾ pound uncolored sharp cheddar cheese, grated or cut up
- ¼ tsp. vitamin C
- 1 tsp. freshly grated nutmeg (from whole nutmeg)
- 1 or 2 potatoes (peeled, cooked and cut into small pieces)
- 1 cup of cream or half and half (unboiled is fine)
- salt (pure variety)

Bring all to a boil. After a minute turn the burner to low, cover pan with a lid and cook slowly for at least 20 minutes.

Sanitation of meats is quick and easy now that freezing and ozonation are available to penetrate deep into the interior. Safety from chlorox bleach treatment can be found by testing with a Syncrometer®. But the extra dyes used everywhere now and unsaturated oils dispersed in the meat create almost unsolvable problems. USA animals have been fed unsaturated oils, gallate-sprayed grains and given chlorox-bleached water to drink, like their owners.

Heightened parasitism is seen in chickens and beef. The animals seem sickly, judging by frequent antibiotic use (read the ads in animal feed stores), and not fit for consumption even by a healthy person. Four kinds of free-range raised (vegetarian) animals did not show these weaknesses:

(1) free-range, organic turkey
(2) free-range lamb
(3) free-range beef (test for Macracanthorhynchus, prions and gold)
(4) buffalo

Bone Marrow-Beef Broth

- **3 or 4 beef bones (cut to expose the bone marrow)**
- **½ lb. of a cheaper cut of beef, including sinews, gristle, cartilage**
- **1 bay leaf**
- **sodium-potassium salt (to taste)**
- **5 drops HCl (5%, USP)**

Place bones and meat in original package in sonicator, on food zapper or zappicator for five minutes. Place meat in large enamel pot. Save bones for later addition. Cover with cold water. Add 5 drops HCl. This will preserve the natural L-G and L-A in the meat. Bring to boil. Remove and discard foam that develops at first during cooking, using wooden spoon.

Add other ingredients and cook till done (about 1 hour). Add bones and cook five minutes more. Add 5 more drops of HCl. Cool. Eat some bone marrow as soon as cool enough. Pour off the broth. Drink one cup a day. Refrigerate. If fat solidifies at the top, do not throw this away. It belongs with the broth. Reheat it daily so it can be mixed.

Variations: Add a homegrown tomato instead of HCl.

Something Sour

Use citric acid and vitamin C to give sour taste to foods. Safe vinegar is fine, but can't be used in colon and prostate cancer.

Citric Tangerine Dessert

- **2 tangerines**
- **2 citric acid capsules or ¼ tsp.**
- **1 tsp. safe sweetener**
- **heavy whipping cream without lactose (optional)**

Hot wash tangerines and save peels in freezer. They have health value. Place tangerines in zippered plastic bag or non-seeping container (no need to disinfect). Add citric acid and sweetener. Mash and mix with stainless steel whip or roll over the bag with a glass jar. Top with cream.

Variations: Boil tangerines with equal amount of water; add other ingredients. Serve on blended foods to provide flavor.

Lettuce A'la Crème – A TV Snack

- **the greenest head lettuce you can find, with many loose outer leaves**
- **2 citric acid capsules or ¼ tsp.**
- **¼ cup heavy whipping cream, sterilized**

Peel away many loose lettuce leaves to get away from adhering radon and sprays. Dip head in Lugol's water for 3 minutes. Add citric acid to whipping cream in a HDPE bowl. Tear pieces of lettuce off the head (don't cut) and dip into the sour cream.

Variations: Use Romaine lettuce or Bok Choy. Add 1 Brazil nut or 4 Hazel nuts, ground.

Spice Mix

- 1 tsp. coriander seeds (frozen)
- 1 tsp. cardamom seeds (frozen)
- 1 tsp. anise seeds (frozen)

Grind 3 seconds; then let grinder blades cool and grind another 3 seconds. Store in freezer to keep potency.

Spice Mix Straight

These spices (above) can be chewed whole; no grinding needed if your teeth are up to it. Adding sweetener or whipping cream makes it a dessert to be nibbled on for hours. A few detox symptoms next day will be a real reward.

Desserts

Coconut Whipping Cream

- "meat" of 1 coconut (with brown skin removed)
- "milk" of 1 coconut

Place meat in blender for 4 seconds only. Then add ¼ cup "milk" and blend another 4 seconds. Continue adding bits of milk till consistency is perfect for you.

Chewy Barley Pearls

- ¼ cup pearled barley (unbrominated)
- water to cover
- sweetening
- spice

Place sanitized barley and water in HDPE bowl and cover. Next morning drain liquid. Add sweetener. Eat straight. Save liquid to drink with spice.

Barley Flakes

(tested for bromine & chlorox)

   Add 1½ times as much water as flakes and let stand overnight in the refrigerator or 2 hours at room temperature. Serve with whipping cream and chopped fruit.

Tapioca - Barley Pudding

   Put into a 2 quart pan.
- **1½ cups water**
- **⅓ cup small tapioca pearls**
- **1½ teaspoons whole barley (grind first for 3 seconds)**
- **Soak the above for one hour, then add:**
- **1⅓ cups water**
- **2 cups heavy whipping cream**
- **½ to ⅔ cup safe sweetener (optional)**
- **¼ to ⅓ cup pure maple syrup (optional)**

   Bring to a boil and let boil for only one minute, stirring constantly with a stainless steel spoon. *Optional*: Add contents of two nutmeg capsules and a tsp. of the spice mix below. Serve warm or cold. Makes approximately eight 4 oz. servings. *NOTE*: For thinner consistency use ½ cup more water.

Brazil Nut Split

(for organic germanium and selenium)

- **1 whole nut in the shell**
- **sturdy nutcracker**
- **1 frozen banana**
- **whipping cream (heavy, kosher, disinfected)**

   Crack the nut when you are ready to use it. Choose a different nut if it is discolored or doesn't taste good after nibbling. Scrape away blemishes. Place frozen banana on stainless steel platter or HDPE dish. Dribble whipping cream over the banana. Before it freezes sprinkle ground Brazil nut over cream. Grind it by pounding in a plastic zippered bag or rolling it with a jar. All nuts have germanium and selenium, but eating more than one large nut a day challenges your digestion of linolenic acid too much so viruses can thrive.

Variations: Add ground rose hips for organic vitamin C.

Santa Split

- **1 large or 2 small frozen bananas**
- **¼ cup heavy whipping cream (kosher)**
- **1 tsp. anise seed (stored in freezer)**

Place banana in HDPE bowl. While frozen, pour on whipping cream. Before it freezes, sprinkle on anise seed.

Variations: 1 tsp. frozen tangerine peel. It is easy to decorate with these spices to form a snowman.

Baked Apples

Peel and core. Remove all bruises. Cut in pieces, add a minimum of water and cook or bake minimally. Add a squirt of lemon juice when done. Serve with cinnamon, whipping cream and honey.

Lettuce - Nut Salad

Use Romaine lettuce or Bok Choy. These need sanitizing after removing outer leaves. A 5 minute dip in Lugol's water or the routine ozonation is enough.

- **lettuce (1 head)**
- **1 Brazil nut or 4 Hazel nuts**
- **¼ cup heavy whipping cream**
- **2 capsules citric acid**
- **sodium-potassium salt (optional)**

Tear the lettuce into tiny pieces. Add citric acid to cream in a HDPE bowl. Pour over the lettuce. Sprinkle on the pounded or ground nuts (grind or pound nuts by hand or with a jar or a can rolled over the nuts in a zippered bag).

Cottage Cheese Cake

This is an excellent way to get more protein into your diet, especially important if you are mostly vegetarian.
- **1 cup cottage cheese (dry variety)**
- **1 egg**
- **1 tsp. honey or confectioner's sugar**
- **1 tsp. butter**
- **cinnamon**

If dry cottage cheese is not available, drain the regular variety. The dryer the cottage cheese the chewier the cheese cake gets. But if you prefer a custard-like consistency, you could use the regular 4% cream cottage cheese without draining; simply blend it for smoothness.

Mix all ingredients and pour into a small glass pie pan with or without a pie shell. Do not use graham crackers or ready-made crust. Sprinkle heavily with cinnamon. Bake at 350° till firm and slightly browned, about 15 to 20 minutes.

Cold Delights

5-Minute Raspberry Ice Cream

Why buy ready made ice cream when homemade is twice as delicious?
- **1 pint heavy whipping cream (previously treated with ¼ capsule lactase enzyme for several hours and then ozonated)**
- **1 carton raspberries (from a farmers' market, disinfected by deep freezing after rinsing)**
- **wheat germ (freshly opened, frozen)**
- **½ cup safe sweetener**
- **nuts (optional)**

Dump frozen raspberries into blender. Pour whipping cream and sweetener over them. Blend for 4 seconds (only). Pour it all into a stainless steel bowl, already chilled in freezer. Don't clean the blades. Quickly sprinkle wheat germ or ground nuts over the top. Cover with close fitting zippered bag and place in freezer. Prepare it a day ahead. Try using other frozen fruit like blueberries, peaches, but not strawberries. Strawberries are very heavily fertilized now with very radioactive fertilizer. In fact, when you dry strawberries (or oranges or purple grapes) they can be tested with a handheld inexpensive Geiger Mueller counter and found to be 10% or more radioactive than the background level. Raspberries have a special anti-cancer factor, **ellagic** acid, as do Brazil nuts. Freeze many pints.

Pear Slush

- **1 large pear**
- **1 Tbsp. safe sweetener**
- **1/8 tsp. citric acid**
- **1 Tbsp. water**

Sterilize in Lugol's water or ozonate. Peel and cut away the stem and flower end, leaving no blemishes. Place in blender with sweetener, water, citric acid, seeds and all (pear seeds are powerful virus killers). Blend 4 seconds (only). Scoop into chilled stainless steel sherbet servers and freeze inside a zippered bag. Serve frozen.

Variations: Add topping of pounded or rolled nuts and whipping cream. *NOTE*: Use any other raw fruit desired, but always add the citric acid.

5-Minute Strawberry Ice Cream

(Strawberry) Use 2 half-pints of whipping cream, previously boiled, 1 package of frozen strawberries (about 10 oz.), and ½ cup clover honey. Pour frozen strawberries into blender. Pour whipping cream and honey over them. Blend briefly (about 10 seconds), not long enough to make butter! Pour it all into a large plastic bowl. Cover with a close fitting plastic bag and place in freezer. Prepare it a day ahead. Try using other frozen fruits, such as blueberries and cherries. Keep a few berries out of the blender and stir them in quickly with a non-metal spoon before setting the bowl in the freezer. There are many ice cream recipes to be found in old cook books. Avoid those with raw eggs or processed foods as ingredients. You may add nuts if you rinse them in vitamin C water.

> ICE CREAMS... from the grocery store are loaded with benzene and other solvents. Fortunately there are ice cream makers that do everything (no cranking)! Or try our recipe which uses a blender. Be sure not to add store bought flavors, except vanilla or maple.

Cookies, Cakes & Pies

Bake cookies, cakes and pies from scratch, using unprocessed ingredients. Use simple recipes from old cook books.

Do not use paper cupcake cups, the wax coating has benzene. Do not use aluminum baking pans, bowls, measuring spoons, or foil wrapping. Do not use stretchable plastic film. Do not use plastic or wood utensils; use stainless steel. Plasticware can be hardened in boiling water for 30 minutes. Use aluminum-free baking powder, pure salt, and butter instead of oils.

Use flour that is not brominated; bromine attracts polonium to be stored in the spleen.

Teas for Pleasure & Health

Hydrangea Tea

(for organic germanium)

- ½ cup hydrangea root, (c/s), organic, frozen
- 3 cups water
- stainless steel strainer

Soak the sterilized dried roots at least 4 hours to get the maximum goodness out of them later. Then simmer for ½ hour at low heat in a stainless steel pan. Let cool and strain into a HDPE container for storage. Several sips provide one dose of germanium for the 2-*Week Program*. Add sweetener to taste. Keep sterile by reheating daily.

Wheat Germ Tea

- 3 heaping tsp. wheat germ
- 1 cup water (plus 1 drop HCl)

Boil wheat germ in water for 1 minute. Strain, drink hot or cold. Save solids to add to other cooked cereal. This beverage draws cobalt, aluminum and antimony into the urine. Drink only 1 cup a day.

Healthy Recipes

Rose Hips Tea

(for organic vitamin C)

- **1 tsp. rose hips (coarse ground, with seeds, organic, frozen)**
- **1 cup water**
- **sweetener or heavy whipping cream (sterilized)**

Bring water to a boil in stainless steel saucepan. Add rose hips, cover, and then remove from heat. When cool pour into safe cup and drink right away. This can replace one dose of the capsules plus a vitamin C capsule in the program. You may add sweetener or whipping cream to taste.

Burdock Tea

This is called an herb, but it is too delicious and flavorful for this simple label.

- **2 Tbsp. burdock root, organic (c/s)**
- **1¼ cups water**

Bring water to boil in stainless steel saucepan. Add burdock and turn down heat to simmer, covered. Simmer for about 20 min. Cool. While it is cooling, it will turn sweetish, and the grounds will settle. Then you can pour it off without a strainer. It is so good straight, nothing needs to be added. Even the "grounds" are good, spooned up with cream or sweetening. Do not make herb teas in the microwave. Some organic germanium would get destroyed and phenolics that should be destroyed would escape. Burdock fights E. coli and more. Sterilize first.

Coconut Tea

- **½ cup shredded coconut or flakes**
- **2 cups water (plus 2 drops HCl)**
- **2 tsp. honey**

Bring coconut and water to a boil, simmering 20 minutes. Press as much as possible through coarse sieve.

Eucalyptus Tea

This tea is too flavorful to be considered an herbal tea, more so if you can pick it off the tree! Best of all is to find that it cures your flu's, Salmonella attacks and even malaria. Most important...it does not need to be tested for thallium or other pesticide. There are several varieties. Gather:

- **5 long leaves or 10 short-variety leaves**
- **2 inches of twig (that holds the leaves)**
- **a marble size piece of bark (if available)**

Rinse under faucet and place in stainless steel pan. Add 2¼ cups water. Bring to a boil, covered. Then turn down heat to simmer for 10 minutes. Cool. Notice the beautiful red color it develops and delicious aroma. You may add whipping cream. During a cold or cough, sip it throughout the day for 2 days (if it lasts that long). It is the only herb, besides oregano (oil) that I have found can kill Clostridium bacteria. Be sure to sterilize every bit.

There are many other herbs used to improve health, discussed in this book. Make these as teas if you have chills or sore throat, adding whatever makes them enjoyable. Do not combine them with other herbs unless they are traditionally combined. They could destroy each other. You need the extra liquid, besides, to stimulate more urine flow.

Although I advised sterilizing them I have never found Salmonella or E. coli bacteria on growing leaves, even if there is dust and the branches hang over streets.

Bone Healer Tea

- **Irish moss (Chondrus crispus)**
- **Comfrey root (Symphytum officinale)**
- **Mullein leaf (Verbascum thapsus)**
- **Burdock root (*Arctium lappa*)**

Combine herbs in equal amounts. Add one half cup of the combined herbs to three cups of water. Let stand at least three hours or overnight. Bring to a boil. Turn burner down to low; cook for 20 minutes. Strain and let tea cool. Boil again for 5 minutes. Add sweetening and two drops HCl per cup at time of serving. Drink ½ cup with each meal.

Lung Tea

These are the traditional herbs for ravaged lungs. Both herbs are often maligned as dangerous or toxic. Hundreds or thousands of years of simple use, as in this recipe speak otherwise. The <u>concentrates</u> of these herbs should, of course, be evaluated differently.

- **¼ cup comfrey root (*Symphytum officinale*)**
- **¼ cup mullein leaf (*Verbascum thapsus*)**
- **3 cups water**

Combine dry herbs with water. Bring to a boil. Turn burner down to low; cook for 20 minutes. Strain and let tea cool. Add sweetening and two drops HCl per cup at time of serving. Drink ½ cup with each meal, sometimes hot, sometimes cool.

Detox-Tea

Prion protein is present in all of us, repeatedly, as our hypothalamus gland becomes inflamed and releases free cells in the blood and lymph. If there is not enough pepsin to digest them, the remains turn into prions. These results are tentative. The true source is not yet certain. Our WBCs eat prions promptly. But if our WBCs do not have enough germanium, selenite, and vitamin C, the prions are not killed but escape and enter the brain and nerves. Light headedness and disorientation is felt. That contributes to detox-illness. You can kill them in hours with:

- 1 tsp. fennel seed (freshly ground, use capsules)
- 1 tsp. sage, organic (freshly ground)
- 3 heaping tsp. birch bark
- 1 Tbsp. sweetener
- 3 cups water

Birch bark is the strongest prion killer and could be used alone. Make birch bark tea by adding to boiling water and then simmering for 5 minutes. Add other ingredients to the birch bark tea. Set to cool. Drink 1 to 3 cups a day till symptoms stop.

Variation: Reishi mushroom, unboiled, instead of birch bark. Make fennel-sage tea. Let cool; add 1 tsp. Reishi, also called Ganoderma.

Buski Tea

- 1 tsp. anise seeds
- 1 tsp. coriander seeds
- 1 tsp. fennel seeds
- 2 cups water
- ½ tsp. whole cloves
- 4 capsules nutmeg
- 2 cups barley water
- sweetener

Make barley water recipe first and refrigerate. Add seeds to water and simmer 10 minutes. Add cloves and remove from heat. When cool, add cold barley water, nutmeg and sweetener. Refrigerate. Strain 1 cup to drink and put back solids. Next day, repeat. On 3rd and 4th day, eat the solids, with extra sweetener if desired. This tea reaches leftover Fasciolopsis in "unreachable" places like eye muscles, jawbone, spine.

Health Recipes

Beverages for Health

Moose Elm Drink

(also known as Slippery Elm)

For sensitive stomachs when nothing wants to stay down:
- **1 tbs. moose elm powder**
- **cold (boiled) milk**

Start by making a paste as if it were cocoa. Gradually add milk, water or whipping cream to consistency desired. Sweeten with confectioner's sugar or honey. This is very like cocoa; can be drunk hot or cold. Sip one cup a day.

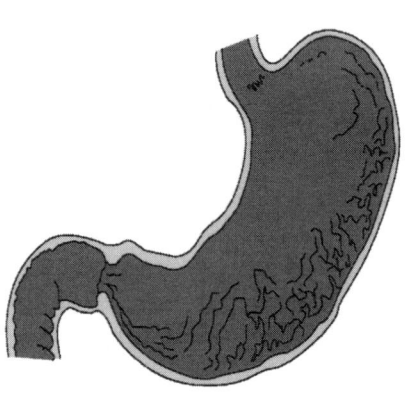

Alginate/Intestinal Healer

For intestines sore from surgery, blockage, or inflammation. This beverage is not meant to be digested; it forms a gelatinous ribbon through the intestine, giving bulk and absorbing toxins along the way. Take 1 cup a day in tablespoon amounts added to soup, stew, pudding, pie, or bouillon.

Bring 2 tsp. sodium alginate powder and 1 pint water to a boil. Stir with wooden spoon handle. Use slow heat – it could take an hour. Add to soup, stew, moose elm beverage, pudding or pie. Consume one to two cups per day.

Raw Bitters

- **one small handful foraged greens**
- **½ cup water**
- **1 tbs. black cherry concentrate**
- **1 pinch vitamin B2**
- **2 drops HCl to sterilize**

Get a book from the library to identify edible varieties. Poisonous plants, like mistletoe or jimson weed or morning glory are rare. If you can't find a book, start with dandelion-like plants, thistles of all kinds, lettuce-like and spinach-like plants. Wild mustard is easy to identify, as are common "weeds" like plantain, chicory, shepherds' purse, cheese plant, lambs quarters. Choose the most perfect leaves, near the top, and also the growing tip. Two leaves, a growing tip and a flower give you four specimens. Five plants give you the handful you need. Sterilize in plastic bowl with Lugol's or HCl-water, stirring well to open any air pockets. Place in blender. Add water. Blend. Add cherry concentrate and B_2 and blend again. Add 2 drops HCl and drink as soon as light treated.

Variations: add a capsule of ginger or turmeric for flavor.

Raw Liver Cocktail

- **¼ slice raw beef liver (about 2" x 2") freshly purchased**
- **$1/16$ tsp. pure salt**

Blend with ½ cup water. Strain. Add 4 drops HCl and light treat. Drink at once.

Additions:
- **An equal volume of cherry concentrate**
- **2 tbs. vinegar**
- **2 drops wintergreen oil**

Pomegranate Seed Drink

- **1 pomegranate (refrigerated)**

Sanitize with Lugol's water. Cut in quarters. Then peel. Place seeds in blender. Blend 10 seconds at a time if fruit is cold, till seeds are fine enough to drink (about 8 sessions). Refrigerated fruit keeps blades cooler. The peel is also medicinal. It eliminates E. recurvatum.

Shark Cartilage

Shark cartilage tastes awful to me, so here are six different ways to take it. If you are taking papain, which tastes (actually, smells) even worse, you could combine it also, on the theory that bad tastes neutralize each other!

RECIPE #1

- 1 tbs. shark cartilage
- ¼ cup cold water
- 1 capsule fenuthyme
- 1 tbs. vinegar

RECIPE #2

- 1 tbs. shark cartilage
- 2 or 3 capsules betaine
- ¼ cup cold water
- ½-1 tsp. turmeric
- 1 tbs. vinegar

RECIPE #3

- 1 tbs. shark cartilage
- ¼ cup beet juice or puree
- 1 tbs. vinegar

RECIPE #4

- 1 tbs. shark cartilage
- 1 tsp. honey
- 1 capsule fennel
- 1 capsule ginger

RECIPE #5
(if dairy allowed)

- 2 tbs. shark cartilage
- 2 capsules fennel
- ½ cup buttermilk

RECIPE #6
(if dairy allowed)

- 2 tbs. shark cartilage
- 2 capsules fennel
- ½ cup milk
- 1 tsp. vitamin C

Shark cartilage should be sterilized to kill bacteria. Add 2 drops of hydrochloric acid to each recipe just before drinking. Stir until smooth. Increase water or vinegar to taste.

Parasite Killer Recipes

Spice Syrup

These are essential oils made from traditional herbs. The herbs have been used for centuries to prevent illness associated with food—and are used to this day, in less developed countries, hence their use as spices. By combining them we get an anti-parasite, anti-bacterial, even anti-viral effect. All of these invaders enter us with food, and can be conquered with food, namely spices.

- **1 tsp. peppermint oil**
- **1 tsp. clove oil**
- **½ tsp. white thyme oil**
- **1 tsp. coriander oil**
- **1 tsp. nutmeg oil**
- **1 tsp. fennel oil**
- **½ cup maple syrup (boiled)**

Mix in glass bottle with enough room to shake. SHAKE VERY WELL before use to prevent separation of oil. If you don't, the bottom portion will not have potency.

The dose is ¼ tsp. 2 times daily. Measure accurately. Do not mix with water. Tip the spoon at the back of tongue and swallow quickly. Chase with a bit of bread until you are used to it. For children: $^1/_8$ tsp. once a day.

General Spice Syrup Recipe

(This is not a single recipe; it is the design for all spice syrups, to make them strong enough but not toxic.)

HEALTHY RECIPES

- **1 tsp. of any mild-flavored spice oil or**
- **½ tsp. strong-flavored spice oil, such as wintergreen, white thyme, frankincense, myrrh**
- **2 to 4 tbsp. pomegranate paste or juice, molasses or chlorophyll**
- **½ cup maple syrup, agave, oil, or honey**

Choose up to 8 spice oils to combine with other ingredients and syrup. A final dose of ¼ tsp. will give you 1 drop of each mild spice and ½ drop of each strong spice. Do not use more than that three times per day. Too much of any one oil could be toxic.

Choose the herbs to suit your needs. Then measure the correct amounts into a pint jar. Add syrup and shake.

Maple syrup must be brought to a boil first and cooled. You may use agave syrup instead of maple syrup, but add 1 tbsp. water too, to help it mix. You may use an oil instead of syrup as the base. If you use honey instead of syrup you may also need 1 tbsp. water to help it mix.

Spice Tea

- **1 tsp. cloves (whole)**
- **1 tsp. barley (whole)**
- **1 tsp. coriander seed**
- **1 tsp. anise (ground)**
- **1 tsp. cardamom (ground)**
- **1 tsp. turmeric (powder)**
- **1 tsp. fennel seed (ground)**
- **¾ tsp. nutmeg (ground)**
- **2½ cups water**

Add all ingredients to water in a non-metal saucepan and simmer 20 minutes. Strain one cupful through plastic strainer and return the solids to the saucepan; refrigerate.

Add a safe sweetening to the cup of tea. Sip over 1 to 2 hours. This is one day's portion. <u>Do not drink more than 1 cup daily</u>. Next day, strain another cupful and sip as before, hot or cold.

Next day, add a cup of water to the saucepan then reboil for 5 minutes to yield a third cup of tea. Finally, you may eat the solids, one-half portion in one day.

This tea replaces the same spices taken as spice syrup. You may add other spices or hide supplements in this tea. This tea kills a variety of parasites, bacteria and viruses. It can also activate the liver to produce a green bowel movement. Even "gallstones" may appear.

Prion Punch

Prion protein is in all of us repeatedly as our bodies kill flu viruses. Our WBCs eat them promptly. But if a lot of flu virus emerges after killing large flukes and many make their way to the brain, they release their own prions and light-headedness and disorientation is felt. That contributes to detox-illness. You can kill them in hours with:

- **2 horseradish capsules**
- **1 tsp. fennel seed (freshly ground)**
- **1 tsp. sage (freshly ground)**
- **3 heaping tsp. birch bark (powdered)**
- **1 tbsp. syrup**

Make birch bark tea by simmering in 3 cups water for 1 minute. Cool. Blend dry ingredients in the birch bark tea and syrup. Drink 1 to 3 cups a day to stop detox-illness.

Paragonimus Punch

By killing Paragonimus in different ways you reach them in different places. Note how vulnerable they are. You do not need all of these. Each herb kills some.

- 1 tsp. hydrangea powder
- 1 tsp. cloves (freshly ground)
- 1 tsp. nutmeg powder
- 7 capsules wormwood (200-300 mg per capsule)
- 3 drops wintergreen oil
- 3 drops sage oil (Clary)
- 3 drops peppermint oil
- 3 drops juniper oil
- 3 drops frankincense
- 3 drops coriander oil
- 3 drops cardamom oil
- 1 tbsp. pomegranate paste or 3 tbsp. juice
- 1 tbsp. chlorophyll liquid
- 6 oz. tea made from Pau d' Arco bark
- 6 oz. tea made from mullein leaf

Place the powders in a tall glass. Add the drops of herbal oils. Then add the liquids, while stirring, to make an enjoyable beverage. Add coconut cream to give a smoother taste. If it is not sweet enough, add agave syrup, honey or boiled maple syrup. Treat each item electronically or the final beverage.

All oils can be substituted with 1 tsp. powder of the same herb.

If you are missing some ingredients, simply leave them out. Add them later when you do have them.

Drink this once a day in divided doses while on this program. Then cut the dosages in half and later in quarters when you are much healthier. Leave out anything you don't tolerate well.

Pau D'Arco has several other names, including Lapacho and Taheebo.

If some of these herbs are already being taken in the Spice Syrup, you may omit them here.

Six Fresh Seeds

- **6 large prunes** or **6 large peaches**
- **6 large apples** or **6 large pears**
- **or 6 nectarines**

Remove the pits or seeds, saving the fruit for other uses.

To crack open pits: find a rock or piece of cement brick. Slide it into a zippered baggie. Position it in your sink over the drain. Or, if you are near a cement sidewalk, slip the 6 pits into a zippered plastic bag. Procure a hammer. After cracking the pits, remove the seeds and place in grinder. If you are very sick choose seeds the size of your thumbnail. In the case of apple or pear seeds, use up to 30 seeds. Add:

- **3 tsp. wheat germ**
- **¼ tsp. nutmeg**
- **¼ tsp. barley flour or ground barley**

Grind 1 tbsp. whole barley first in coffee grinder and store. Then grind all ingredients together. Eat within a few hours. The barley, like the wheat germ, provides the drying effect that keeps fresh seeds from clogging the grinder.

Variation: add 1 tsp. sweetened coconut.

It is thought that amygdalin or "laetrile" is the active ingredient, but there is no evidence for this since clinical trials got stalled decades ago after finding it promising against cancer. Amygdalin keeps its potency; the active ingredient we seek does not.

Apricot kernels in health food stores have lost their potency so you must prepare your own. Do not crack these pits ahead of time nor store seeds, although you may store pits. The correct amount is essential for us but large amounts are toxic, somewhat like trace elements. Do not take more. Six Fresh Seeds can kill SV40 and Fasciolopsis buski, as well as destroying many phenolics.

The dose is one set of 6 kernels or the seeds of six fruits daily for 6 days, then take 6 days off and repeat the cycle till you are much better.

Parasite-Killing Program

1. Black Walnut Hull Tincture Extra Strength

Day 1: (this is the day you begin; start the same day you receive it).

Take one drop. Put it in ½ cup of water. Sip it on an empty stomach such as before a meal.

Day 2: take two drops in ½ cup water same as above.

Day 3: take three drops in ½ cup water same as above.

Day 4: take four drops in ½ cup water same as above.

Day 5: take five drops in ½ cup water same as above.

Day 6: take 2 tsp. all together in ½ cup water or added to lemonade, or EZ Meal. Sip it; don't gulp it. Get it down within 15 minutes. If you are over 150 pounds, take 2½ tsp. You may add honey, spices or syrup to flavor.

This dose kills most *Fasciolopsis buski* throughout the body. But it does not reach locations under the skin or far away in the genitals or brain. We will use apricot seeds and watercress tablets for these. The alcohol in the tincture can make you slightly woozy for several minutes. Simply stay seated until you are comfortable again. Then take niacinamide, 500 mg, to counteract the toxicity of the alcohol. You could also feel a slight nausea for a few minutes. Walk in the fresh air or rest until it passes.

> Family members and friends should take 2 tsp. every other week to avoid reinfecting you. They may be harboring a few parasite stages in their intestinal tract without having symptoms.

For a year take 2 tsp. Black Walnut Hull Tincture Extra Strength every week or until your HIV or AIDS is but a dim memory. For advanced AIDS you will need this much daily. Do not substitute any powdered variety until you are much better.

You may be wondering why you should wait for five days before taking the 2 tsp. dose. It is for your convenience only.

HEALTHY RECIPES

You may have a sensitive stomach or be worried about toxicity or side effects. By the sixth day you will have convinced yourself that there are no toxic side effects.

Going faster. In fact, if you are convinced after the first drop of the beneficial action of Black Walnut Hull Tincture, take the 2 tsp. dose on the very first day. You may take 2 tsp. daily after that if you wish.

Going slower. On the other hand, if you cringe at the thought of taking an herb or you are anxious about its safety, continue the drops, increasing at your own pace, until you are ready to brave the decisive 2 tsp. dose.

2. Wormwood capsules (should contain 200-300 mg of wormwood:

Day 1: take 1 capsule before supper (with water).
Day 2: take 1 capsule before supper.
Day 3: take 2 capsules before supper.
Day 4: take 2 capsules before supper.

Continue increasing in this way to day 14, whereupon you are up to 7 capsules. You take the capsules all in a single dose (but one at a time until they are all gone). Then you do two more days of 7 capsules each. After this, you take 7 capsules once a week forever, as it states in the *Maintenance Parasite Program*. Try not to get interrupted before the 6th day, so you know the adult intestinal flukes are dead. After this, you may proceed more slowly if you wish. Many persons with sensitive stomachs prefer to stay longer on each dose instead of increasing according to this schedule. You may choose the pace after the sixth day.

3. Cloves: Fill size 00 capsules with fresh ground cloves; if this size is not available, use size 0 or 000. In a pinch, empty vitamin capsules. You may be able to purchase fresh ground cloves that are already encapsulated; they should be about 500 mg. Grocery store ground cloves do not work! Grind them yourself.

Day 1: Take 1 capsule, 3 times daily before meals.
Day 2: Take 2 capsules, 3 times daily.
Days 3, 4, 5, 6, 7, 8, 9, 10: Take 3 capsules, 3 times daily.

HEALTHY RECIPES

After day 10: Take 7 capsules all together once a week forever, as in the *Maintenance Parasite Program*.

Alternatively, you may make yourself clove syrup:

- **1 tsp. oil of clove bud**
- **½ cup syrup**

Add together. Shake well each time you are taking a dose. Dose is ¼ tsp. 2 times daily. It is easiest to take this at the back of the tongue, swallowing quickly. Follow with bread, not water until you are used to it.

Take **ornithine** at bedtime for insomnia. Even if you do not suffer from insomnia now, you may when you kill parasites.

TIPS ON TAKING PILLS.

Whenever taking capsules or pills, have a bit of bread within reach. If a pill should stick, swallow some bread. Bread pushes the pill along its way, while water does not. Never take a handful of pills together. They may clump together and give you lots of discomfort. Take them one at a time.

Parasite Program Handy Chart

Day	Black Walnut Hull Tincture Extra Strength Dose drops 1 time per day, like before a meal	Wormwood Capsule Dose (200-300 mg) capsules 1 time per day, on empty stomach (before meal)	Clove Capsule Dose (Size 0 or 00) capsules 3 times per day, like at mealtime
1	1	1	1, 1, 1
2	2	1	2, 2, 2
3	3	2	3, 3, 3
4	4	2	3, 3, 3
5	5	3	3, 3, 3
6	2 tsp.	3	3, 3, 3
7	0	4	3, 3, 3
8	0	4	3, 3, 3
9	0	5	3, 3, 3
10	0	5	3, 3, 3
11	0	6	7
12	0	6	0
13	2 tsp.	7	0
14	0	7	0
15	0	7	0
16	0	7	0
17	0	0	0
18	0	0	7
19	now 2 tsp. once a week (or 5 capsules)	now 7 capsules once a week	now 7 capsules once a week

At this point you do not need to keep a strict schedule, but instead may choose any day of the week to take all the parasite program ingredients.

Continue on the *Maintenance Parasite Program*, indefinitely, to prevent future reinfection.

Maintenance Parasite Program

You are always picking up parasites! Parasite eggs are everywhere around you! You get them from other people, your family, yourself, your home, your pets, undercooked meat, uncooked dairy products and hidden dirt on fruits and vegetables.

I believe the <u>main</u> source of the intestinal fluke is <u>undercooked dairy products and meats</u>. After we are infected with it this way, we can give it to each other through blood, saliva, semen, and breast milk, which mean kissing on the mouth, sex, nursing, and childbearing.

Family members nearly always have the same parasites. If one person develops HIV or cancer, the others probably have the intestinal fluke also. They should give themselves the same deparasitizing program.

Do this once a week. Space them as close together as you comfortably can so it becomes a single treatment.

- **Black Walnut Hull Tincture Extra Strength:** 2 tsp. on an empty stomach, like before a meal or bedtime OR **5 capsules of Black Walnut Hull (freeze-dried)**
- **Wormwood capsules:** 7 capsules (with 200-300 mg wormwood each) together on an empty stomach.
- **Cloves:** 7 capsules (about 500 mg. each) together on an empty stomach. Alternatively, take ¼ tsp. homemade clove syrup 2 times on this day.
- **Take ornithine** every night until you don't need it.

The only after effects you may feel are due to dead parasites! They release their own bacteria and viruses at this time. If this maintenance treatment gives you <u>any</u> noticeable after effects on the same or next day, it means you did indeed kill something. You will know it is gone when there are no after effects from the maintenance dose.

Parasite Essential Foods

Parasite	Food	Killed by
Ascaris lumbricoides, pet roundworm	quercitin (squash & pumpkin, undercooked)	BQ
Ascaris megalocephala, pet roundworm	D-carnitine (meat of domestic animals, not free-range, organic)	RZ
Clonorchis sinensis, human liver fluke	oats, cooked or raw	BWT (Black walnut tincture)
Dirofilaria, dog heartworm	lactose (milk sugar)	levamisole
Echinoporyphium recurvatum	lentils, Nopales, Cu	Glyoxal
Echinostoma revolutum	Zein, sorghum	Glyoxylic acid; 6 Fresh Seeds
Eurytrema pancreaticum, pancreatic fluke	lemon and lauric acid (food oil)	BWT (Black walnut tincture)
Fasciolopsis buski, human intestinal fluke	raw onion (allyl sulfide, diallyl sulfide, allyl methyl sulfide, and other onion-like substances in the lily family)	BWT (Black walnut tincture); 6 Fresh Seeds; zapping
Fasciola	wheat (gluten, gliadin); metacercaria require lauric acid, food oil	
Onchocerca, filaria roundworm	corn, mannitol (sugar), linolenic food oil	Decaris
Paragonimus, lung fluke	lemon	BWT (Black walnut tincture)
Plasmodium falciparum, vivax, malariae (malaria)	different stages need iron disulfide, wheat, lemon, melanin, plantain, ASA, pyrrole, others	avoidance of allergen and benzene
Strongyloides, roundworm	potatoes, raw or cooked, linolenic acid (food oil)	levamisole

HEALTHY RECIPES

Pet Parasite Program

Pets have many of the same parasites that we get, including Ascaris (common roundworm), hookworm, Trichinella, Toxoplasma, Strongyloides, heartworm and various tapeworms. Every pet living in your home should be deparasitized and maintained on a parasite program. Your pet is part of your family and should be kept as sweet and clean and healthy as yourself. This is not difficult to achieve. Here is the recipe:

1. Parsley water: cook a big bunch of fresh parsley in a quart of cold tap water for three minutes. Add four drops hydrochloric acid to detoxify traces of benzene from pesticide residue before cooking. Throw away the parsley. After cooling, you may freeze most of it in several one-cup containers. This is a month's supply. Put 1 tsp. parsley water on the pet's food. You don't have to watch it go down. Whatever amount is eaten is satisfactory.

> All dosages are based on a 10-pound (5 kilo) cat or dog. Double them for a 20-pound pet, and so forth.

Pets are full of parasites, you must be quite careful not to deparasitize too quickly. The purpose of the parsley water is to keep the kidneys flowing well so dead parasite refuse is eliminated promptly. They get quite fond of their parsley water. Perhaps they can sense the benefit it brings them. Do this for a week before starting the Black Walnut Hull tincture.

2. Black Walnut hull tincture (regular strength): one drop on the food. Don't force them to eat it. Count carefully.

HEALTHY RECIPES

Treat cats only twice a week. Treat dogs daily, for instance a 30-pound dog would get three drops per day (but work up to it, increasing one drop per day). Do not use Extra Strength.

If your pet vomits or has diarrhea, you may expect to see worms. Never let a child clean up a pet mess. Finally, clean your hands with diluted grain alcohol (dilute 1 part alcohol with 4 parts water). Grain alcohol is actually *ethyl* alcohol that has been made by fermenting grain. In some countries sugar cane is used to make ethyl alcohol. A common brand in the US is Everclear™. But be careful. The smaller flask sizes are polluted with solvents from the pumping and filling processes, no doubt. Choose the 750 ml or 1 liter bottle, which is evidently bottled differently. Be careful to keep all alcohol out of sight of children; don't rely on discipline for this. Be careful not to buy isopropyl rubbing alcohol for this purpose.

Start the wormwood a week later.

3. Wormwood capsules: (200-300 mg wormwood per capsule) open a capsule and put the smallest pinch possible on their dry food. Do this for a week before starting the cloves.

4. Cloves: put the smallest pinch possible on their dry food. Keep all of this up as a routine so that you need not fear your pets. Also, notice how peppy and happy they become.

Go slowly so the pet can learn to eat all of it. To repeat:
Week 1: parsley water
Week 2: parsley water and Black Walnut
Week 3: parsley water, Black Walnut, and wormwood
Week 4: parsley water, Black Walnut, wormwood, and cloves

See the following handy chart.

Week	Parsley Water	BWT Tincture	Wormwood Capsule	Clove Capsule
	teaspoons on food	drops on food, cats twice per week, dogs daily	open capsule, put smallest pinch on food	open capsule, put smallest pinch on food
1	1 or more, based on size			
2	1 or more	1		
3	1 or more	1 or more, based on size	1	
4	1 or more	1 or more	1	1
5 and on	1 or more	1 or more	1	1

Pets should not stroll on counters or table. They should eat out of their own dishes, not yours. They should not sleep on your bed. The bedroom should be off limits to pets. Don't kiss your pets. Wash your hands after playing with your pet.

NEVER, NEVER share food with your pet. Don't keep a cat box in the house; install a cat door. If you have a sandbox for the children, buy new sand from a lumberyard and keep it covered. Don't eat in a restaurant where they sweep the carpet while you are eating (the dust has parasite eggs tracked in from outside). Never let a child crawl on the sidewalk or the floor of a public building. Wash children's hands before eating. Eat "finger" foods with a fork. If feasible, leave shoes at the door.

Safe pet food is hard to find; traces of solvents in their food are just as bad for your pet as it is for you. Don't buy flavored or colored pet foods. They are polluted with solvents such as carbon tetrachloride, benzene, isopropyl alcohol, wood alcohol, etc. I encourage you to verify this with the Syncrometer® or by sending a sample to an analytical lab.

Pets add a great deal to human lives and should have the same loving care you give yourself.

Organ Improvement Recipes

Kidney Cleanse

- ½ cup dried Hydrangea root
- ½ cup Gravel root
- ½ cup Marshmallow root
- 4 bunches of fresh parsley
- Goldenrod tincture (leave out of recipe if allergic)
- **Ginger capsules**
- **Uva Ursi capsules**
- **Black Cherry Concentrate (8 oz)**
- **Vitamin B6 (250 mg)**
- **Magnesium oxide (300 mg in powder form)**

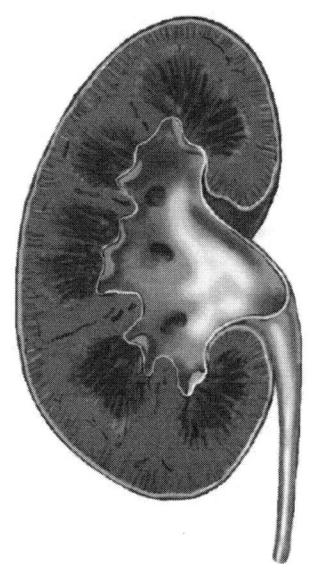

Measure ¼ cup of each root (this is half your supply) and set them to soak, together in 10 cups of cold tap water, using a non-metal container and a non-metal lid (a dinner plate will do). After four hours or overnight, add 8 oz. black cherry concentrate, heat to boiling and simmer for 20 minutes. Drink ¼ cup as soon as it is cool enough. Pour the rest through a bamboo strainer into a sterile pint jar (glass) and several freezable containers. Refrigerate the glass jar.

Find fresh parsley at a grocery store that does not spray its produce (ask the owner). Zappicate the entire supply to be sure it is benzene and PCB-free. Boil the fresh parsley, after rinsing, in 1 quart of water for three minutes. Drink ¼ cup when cool enough. Refrigerate a pint and freeze 1 pint. Throw away the parsley.

Dose: each morning, pour together ¾ cup of the root mixture and ½ cup parsley water, filling a large mug. Add 20 drops of goldenrod tincture. You may flavor with 1 tsp. pomegranate paste, molasses or chlorophyll. Drink this mixture in divided doses throughout the day. Keep cold. <u>Do not drink it all at once</u> or you will get a stomachache and feel pressure in your bladder. If your stomach is very sensitive, start on half this dose.

Save the roots after the first boiling, storing them in the freezer. After 13 days when your supply runs low, boil the same roots a second time, but add only six cups water and simmer only 10 minutes. This will last another eight days, for a total of three weeks. You may cook the roots a third time if you wish, but the recipe gets less potent. If your problem is severe, only cook them twice.

After three weeks, repeat with fresh herbs. You need to do the Kidney Cleanse for six weeks to get good results, longer for severe problems.

Also take:
- **Ginger capsules:** one with each meal (three a day)
- **Uva Ursi capsules:** one with breakfast and two with supper
- **Vitamin B6** (250 mg): one a day
- **Magnesium oxide** (300 mg): one a day

Take these supplements just before your meal to avoid burping. If you are already taking these supplements, omit them here.

Some notes on this recipe: this herbal tea, as well as the parsley, can easily spoil. Heat it to boiling every fourth day if it is being stored in the refrigerator; this resterilizes it. If you sterilize it in the morning you may take it to work without refrigerating it (use a glass container).

When you order your herbs, be careful! Herb companies are not the same! These roots should have a strong fragrance. If the ones you buy are barely fragrant, they have lost their active ingredients; switch to a different supplier. Fresh roots can be used.

Healthy Recipes

- **Hydrangea (*Hydrangea arborescens*) is a common flowering bush.**
- **Gravel root (*Eupatorium purpureum*) is a wild flower.**
- **Marshmallow root (*Althea officinallis*) is mucilaginous and kills pain.**
- **Fresh parsley can be bought at a grocery store. Parsley flakes and dried parsley herb do NOT work.**
- **Goldenrod herb works as well as the tincture but you may get an allergic reaction from smelling the herb. If you know you are allergic to this, leave this one out of your recipe.**
- **Ginger from the grocery store works fine; you may put it into capsules for yourself (size 0, 1 or 00).**

There are probably dozens of herbs that can dissolve kidney crystals and stones. If you can only find several of those in the recipe, make the recipe anyway; it will just take longer to get results. Remember that vitamin B_6 and magnesium, taken daily, can prevent oxalate stones from forming, but only if you stop drinking regular tea. Tea has 15.6 mg oxalic acid per cup. A tall glass of iced tea could give you over 20 mg oxalic acid. Switch to herb teas. Cocoa and chocolate, also, have too much oxalic acid to be used as beverages.

Phosphate crystals are made at locations that are much too alkaline. This happens where bacteria are thriving. They are very hard to dissolve again. The kidneys are quite susceptible to bacteria and "stone" formation. Drink at least two pints of water a day to avoid making more.

> Cleanse your kidneys at least twice a year.

You can dissolve all your kidney stones in three weeks, but make new ones in three days if you are drinking tea and cocoa. Keep bacteria levels down with liver cleanses, betaine and lots of fluid.

Liver Herbs

Don't confuse these liver herbs with the next recipe for the Liver Cleanse. This recipe contains herbs traditionally used to help the liver function, while the Liver Cleanse gets gallstones out.

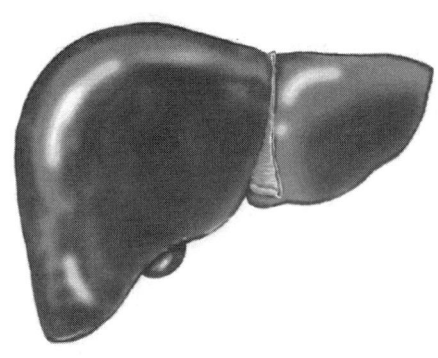

- 6 parts tanner's oak bark, *Quercus alba* (white oak bark)
- 3 parts gravel root, *Eupatorium purpureum* (queen of the meadow)
- 3 parts Jacob's staff, *Verbascum thapsus* (mullein herb)
- 2 parts licorice root, *Glycyrrhiza glabra*
- 2 parts wild yam root, *Dioscorea villosa*
- 2 parts milk thistle herb, *Silybum marianum*
- 3 parts walnut bark, *Juglans nigra* (Black Walnut bark)
- 3 parts marshmallow root, *Althea officinalis* (white mallow)
- 1 part lobelia plant, *Lobelia inflata* (bladder pod)
- 1 part skullcap, *Scutellaria lateriflora* (helmet flower)

Mix all the herbs. Add ½ cup of the mixture to two quarts of water. Bring to a boil. Put lid on. Let it sit for six hours. Strain and add sweetening such as Agave syrup or honey. You can make it extra good by adding coconut cream. Drink three cups a day. This gives you about ¼ cup of each herb. Put the strained herbs in the freezer and use them one more time.

Liver Cleanse

Cleansing the liver of gallstones dramatically improves digestion, which is the basis of your whole health. You can expect your allergies to disappear, too, more with each cleanse you do! Incredibly, it also eliminates shoulder, upper arm, and upper back pain. You have more energy and increased sense of well being.

It is the job of the liver to make bile, 1 to 1½ quarts in a day! The liver is full of tubes (*biliary tubing*) that deliver the bile to one large tube (the *common bile duct*). The gallbladder is attached to the common bile duct and acts as a storage reservoir. Eating fat or protein triggers the gallbladder to squeeze itself empty after about 20 minutes, and the stored bile finishes its trip down the common bile duct to the intestine.

> Cleaning the liver bile ducts is the most powerful procedure that you can do to improve your body's health, but it should NOT BE DONE BEFORE the parasite program, and for best results SHOULD FOLLOW the kidney cleanse.

For many persons, including children, the biliary tubing is choked with gallstones. Some develop allergies or hives but some have no symptoms. When the gallbladder is scanned or X-rayed nothing is seen. Typically, they are not in the gallbladder. Not only that, most are too small and not calcified, a prerequisite for visibility on X-ray. There are over half a dozen varieties of gallstones, most of which have cholesterol crystals in them. They can be black, red, white, green or tan colored. The green ones get their color from being coated with bile. Notice in the picture how many have imbedded unidentified objects. Are they fluke remains? Notice how many are shaped like corks with longitudinal grooves below the tops. We can visualize the blocked bile ducts from such shapes. Other stones are composites—made of many smaller ones—

showing that they regrouped in the bile ducts some time after the last cleanse.

At the very center of each stone is found a clump of bacteria, according to scientists, suggesting a dead bit of parasite might have started the stone forming.

As the stones grow and become more numerous the backpressure on the liver causes it to make less bile. It is also thought to slow the flow of lymphatic fluid. Imagine the situation if your garden hose had marbles in it. Much less water would flow, which in turn would decrease the ability of the hose to squirt out the marbles. <u>With gallstones, much less cholesterol leaves the body, and cholesterol levels may rise.</u>

Gallstones, being porous, can pick up all the bacteria, viruses and parasite eggs that are passing through the liver. In this way "nests" of infection are formed, forever supplying the body with fresh parasite eggs and bacteria. No stomach infection such as ulcers or intestinal bloating can be cured permanently without removing these gallstones from the liver.

INGREDIENTS	
Epsom salts	4 tablespoons
Olive oil	½ cup (light olive oil is easier to get down)
Fresh pink grapefruit	1 large or 2 small, enough to squeeze ½ to $^2/_3$ cup juice (you may substitute a lemon, adding water or sweetener to make ½ cup liquid)
Ornithine	4 to 8, to be sure you can sleep. Don't skip this or you may have the worst night of your life!
Large plastic straw	To help drink potion.
Pint jar with lid	
Black Walnut Tincture, any strength OR 2 freeze-dried capsules	10 to 20 drops, to kill parasites coming from the liver.

HEALTHY RECIPES   93

You can't clean a liver with living parasites in it. You won't get many stones, and you may feel quite sick. Zap daily the week before, or get through the first three weeks of the parasite-killing program before attempting a liver cleanse. If you are on the *Maintenance Parasite Program*, you are always ready to do the cleanse.

Completing the kidney cleanse before cleansing the liver is also <u>highly recommended</u>. You want your kidneys, bladder and urinary tract in top working condition so they can efficiently remove any undesirable substances incidentally absorbed from the intestine as the bile is being excreted.

Choose a day like Saturday for the cleanse, since you will be able to rest the next day.

Take <u>no</u> medicines, vitamins or pills that you can do without; they could prevent success. Stop the parasite program and kidney herbs, too, the day before. Even stop zapping and taking drops.

Double hot wash the grapefruit (or lemon). Zappicate the oil to destroy traces of benzene and PCBs or add a few drops HCl and shake.

Eat a <u>no-fat</u> breakfast and lunch such as cooked cereal, fruit, fruit juice, bread and preserves or honey (no butter or milk). This allows the bile to build up and develop pressure in the liver. Higher pressure pushes out more stones. Limit the <u>amount</u> you eat to the minimum you can get by on. You will get more stones. The earlier you stop eating the better your results will be, too.

2:00 PM. <u>Do not eat or drink after 2 o'clock</u>. If you break this rule you could feel quite ill later.

Get your Epsom salts ready. Mix 4 tbsp. in three cups water and pour this into a jar. This makes four servings, ¾ cup each. Set the jar in the refrigerator to get ice cold (this is for convenience and taste only).

6:00 PM. Drink one serving (¾ cup) of the ice-cold Epsom salts. If you did not prepare this ahead of time, mix 1 tbsp. in ¾ cup water now. You may add ⅛ tsp. vitamin C powder to improve the taste. You may also drink a few sips of water afterwards or rinse your mouth.

HEALTHY RECIPES 94

Get the olive oil and grapefruit out to warm up.

8:00 PM. Repeat by drinking another ¾ cup of Epsom salts.

You haven't eaten since two o'clock, but you won't feel hungry. Get your bedtime chores done. The timing is critical for success.

9:45 PM. Pour ½ cup (measured) olive oil into the pint jar. Squeeze the grapefruit (or lemon) by hand into the measuring cup. Remove pulp with fork. You should have at least ½ cup; more (up to ¾ cup) is best. You may top it up with lemonade. Add this to the olive oil. Also, add Black Walnut Tincture or have freeze-dried capsules ready instead. Close the jar tightly and shake hard until watery (only fresh citrus juice does this).

Now visit the bathroom one or more times, even if it makes you late for your ten o'clock drink. Don't be more than 15 minutes late. You will get fewer stones.

10:00 PM. Drink the potion you have mixed. Take 4 ornithine capsules with the first sips to make sure you will sleep through the night. Take eight if you already suffer from insomnia. Drinking through a large plastic straw helps it go down easier. You may use oil and lemon juice salad dressing, cinnamon, or straight honey to chase it down between sips. Take it to your bedside if you want, but drink it standing up. Get it down within five minutes (15 minutes for very elderly or weak persons).

Lie down immediately. You might fail to get stones out if you don't. The sooner you lie down the more stones you will get out. Be ready for bed ahead of time. Don't clean up the kitchen. As soon as the drink is down walk to your bed and lie down flat on your back with your head up high on the pillow. Try to think about what is happening in the liver. Try to keep perfectly still for at least 20 minutes. You may feel a train of stones traveling along the bile ducts like marbles. There is no pain because the bile duct valves are open (thank you Epsom salts!). **Go to sleep**, you may fail to get stones out if you don't.

Next morning. Upon awakening take your third dose of Epsom salts. If you have indigestion or nausea wait until it is gone before drinking the Epsom salts. You may go back to bed. Don't take this potion before 6:00 am.

2 Hours Later. Take your fourth (the last) dose of Epsom salts. You may go back to bed again.

After 2 More Hours you may eat. Start with fruit juice. Half an hour later eat fruit. One hour later you may eat regular but keep it light. During the day take parasite-killing herbs and zap. By supper you should be recovered.

Alternative Schedule 1: Omit the first Epsom salts dose at 6 p.m. Take only one dose, waiting till 8 p.m. Change nothing else. Many people still get stones with one less dose. If you do not, do the full course next time.

Alternative Schedule 2: After taking the first dose of Epsom salts in the morning, wait two hours and take a second dose (but only ½ cup) of the oil mixture and go back to bed. After two more hours take another dose of Epsom salts. This schedule can increase the number of stones you remove.

How well did you do? Expect diarrhea in the morning. This is desirable. Use a flashlight to look for gallstones in the toilet with the bowel movement. Look for the green kind since this is proof that they are genuine gallstones, not food residue. Only bile from the liver is pea green. The bowel movement sinks but gallstones float because of the cholesterol inside. Count them all roughly, whether tan or green. You will need to total 2000 stones before the liver is clean enough to rid you of allergies or bursitis or upper back pains permanently. The first cleanse may rid you of them for a few days, but as the stones from the rear travel forward, they give you the same symptoms again. You may repeat cleanses at two-week intervals. Never cleanse when you are ill.

Sometimes the bile ducts are full of cholesterol crystals that did not form into round stones. They appear as "chaff" floating on top of the toilet bowl water. It may be tan colored, harboring millions of tiny white crystals. Cleansing this chaff is just as important as purging stones.

How safe is the liver cleanse? It is very safe. However it can make you feel quite ill for one or two days afterwards, although in every one of these cases the *Maintenance Parasite*

Program had been neglected. This is why the instructions direct you to complete the parasite and kidney cleanse programs first.

> Cleanse your liver twice a year.

Warning: If you do change these recipes you might expect problems. The liver is quite sensitive to details.

This procedure contradicts many modern medical viewpoints. Gallstones are thought to be formed in the gallbladder, not the liver. They are thought to be few, not thousands. They are not linked to pains other than gallbladder attacks. It is easy to understand why this is thought: by the time you have acute pain attacks, some stones <u>are</u> in the gallbladder, <u>are</u> big enough and sufficiently calcified to see on X-ray, and <u>have</u> caused inflammation there. When the gallbladder is removed the acute attacks are gone, but the bursitis and other pains and digestive problems remain.

> **CONGRATULATIONS!**
> You have taken out your gallstones <u>without surgery</u>! I like to think I have perfected this recipe, but I certainly cannot take credit for its origin. It was invented hundreds, if not thousands, of years ago. THANK YOU, HERBALISTS!

The truth is self-evident. People who have had their gallbladder surgically removed still get plenty of green, bile-coated stones, and anyone who cares to dissect their stones can see that the concentric circles and crystals of cholesterol match textbook pictures of "gallstones" exactly.

Immunity Boosters

Ferritin Fighter

When white blood cells have phagocytized (eaten) asbestos, they become coated on the outside with ferritin. This ruins their immune function. Their outside surface has receptor sites that must be able to "see" and "feel" enemies of your body. Removing this ferritin restores their immune functions. The drug levamisole (available in other countries) can do this in less than a week (50 mg, take two, 3 times daily), but here is a recipe that works also.

- **1 tsp. bromelain (3000 mg) 600 GDU/gm, or papain**
- **1 tsp. powdered hydrangea**
- **1 capsule fennel for flavoring**
- **½ cup water, goat milk, or coconut cream for mixing**
- **2 drops hydrochloric acid to sterilize**

Mix everything together and drink. Take this dose 3 times daily. For convenience, you can mix larger quantities of the dry (not wet) ingredients ahead of time; this reduces the odor. Cut dosage in half after a week. Do not take with meals to avoid consuming the enzymes with food. Continue for a month.

The bromelain or papain will digest the ferritin off your white blood cells, enabling them to remove asbestos, dyes, bacteria, and plastics from your tissues again. But ferritin will return to coat your white blood cells if you continue to eat or drink asbestos-polluted food or water.

Hydrangea is included because most people find it easier to take this way, than by itself. It is not essential.

Watercress (*Nasturtium officinale*) tablets can also remove ferritin. Chew 6 tablets a day.

Dye Remover Syrup

Each of these three herbs can remove azo dyes from CD4 and CD8 cells. Since each item is effective, you do not need to wait to get them all, first.
- **1 tsp. bay oil**
- **2 tbsp. pomegranate paste**
- **1 tsp. lemon oil**
- **½ cup maple syrup (boiled)**

Zappicate each item in its original container for 10 minutes. Combine all ingredients in a glass jar large enough to allow for vigorous shaking. Dose: ¼ tsp. 3 times daily.

Two more herbs can do this:
- **2 tsp. powdered hydrangea**
- **2 tsp. powdered olive leaf**

Take these straight, stirred into a beverage that suits your taste.

Freon Removal Program

Freon accumulates in the diaphragm and skin in healthy persons. In sick persons the Syncrometer® detects it in the weakened organ. Freon in your body can be ozonated to render it capable of detoxification. This mobilizes it toward the liver.
- **1-3 glasses ozonated water. Ozonate water for five minutes. Make sure the tip of the ozonator tube is sterile by dipping in HCl-water or Lugol's-water first.**
- **1-2 cups liver herb tea. Drink ½ cup tea for each glass of ozonated water drunk. This helps the liver detoxify the Freon so it can move toward the kidneys.**
- **kidney herb tea. Drink 1¼ cups daily. This helps the kidneys pull it into the bladder for excretion.**

It takes about six weeks to remove Freon from your body. Be sure to get a Freon-free refrigerator before you begin.

L-A Recipe

- 1 tsp. L-aspartic acid
- 1 tsp. L-lysine powder
- 1 $\frac{1}{3}$ cups water

If you purchase these powders already mixed you will need 2 tsp. for the recipe.

Heat, covered, till completely dissolved; it will be near boiling. Use a non-metal pan and non-metal stirring spoon. If it develops a white crystalline precipitate at the bottom, it must be reheated to get it redissolved. Add enough water to keep it dissolved. Since it has no preservatives, you <u>must</u> reheat it to near boiling every fourth day to kill any growing bacteria.

Dose: take 1 teaspoon 4 times daily (or 2 tsp. twice a day) if you are quite ill. Take on an empty stomach, such as before meals. Take 1 tsp. 3 times daily (if not so ill) for as long as you feel you have a viral condition. There are no side effects. Use a non-metal spoon.

Mechanism of L-A. L-A is present in all our white blood cells. It specifically helps them remove copper, cobalt, vanadium, toxic germanium, toxic selenium, toxic chromate and nickel. This set of metals is our "natural" set; those brought in by bacteria or fungus, as opposed to unnatural ones brought in by amalgam, body products, etc.

L-G Recipe

- 1 tsp. L-glutamic acid powder (not glutamine)
- 1 tsp. L-lysine powder (you may open capsules)
- 1$\frac{1}{3}$ cups water

Prepare as for L-A. Dosage is one tablespoon 4 times daily.

Mechanism of L-G. These two amino acids combine chemically in hot water to make eight or more different dipeptides. Each is a form (isomer) of L-G. L-G travels to your thymus; this much can be observed electronically. Does it help T-cells survive? Does it do some other vital task? Today, 10 years after its discovery, some questions can be answered.

L-G is found normally present in at least ten kinds of white blood cells including lymphocytes, neutrophils, and even eosinophils. The CD4s and CD8s normally kill viruses but without L-G they do not. They seem to fill up on them or attack them but are not able to kill them. All CD4s and other white blood cells that do not have L-G present, <u>have mercury and/or thallium stuck inside them</u>. This is coming from amalgam deposits, located in very many places in the body. You have been robbed of your L-G making ability.

Fortunately, taking L-G, as made in this recipe, helps the CD4s and others to eject their mercury and thallium. Perhaps it is the body's own heavy metal chelator. Now they can kill viruses again and get your body well. If more amalgam comes their way they again fill up on all 50 or so, metals. Most of them can be destroyed or detoxified somehow. Only mercury and thallium cannot, they remain stuck in the lymphocytes and other specialized white blood cells.

Taking repeated doses of L-G can clean up the white blood cells repeatedly but this is only permanent after amalgam has been removed from the whole body. Nevertheless, this can be accomplished in about six weeks, provided there are no amalgam filled teeth still in your mouth.

As soon as L-G returns to the CD4s they manufacture interleukin 2 again, another important immune chemical. When the CD8s get their L-G they begin killing vagrant tissue bits, tumor cells, and virus filled cells. And life is back to normal.

Supplements for Special Purposes

How To Take Supplements

Taking some supplements out of the capsule reduces the queasiness and discomfort from dozens of capsules bouncing around in your stomach. Capsules can be cut in half with scissors and dumped into foods or mixed with straight honey or maple syrup to make "candy". Always add spices (natural herbs only, commercial varieties may have added dyes!) to such a concoction. But you need to be warned which supplements taste like burning rubber tires or worse so you can leave these in their capsules. Here is my assessment of taste.

- **Supplements that taste terrible:** glutathione, methionine, thioctic, amino acids, niacinamide, papain.
- **Supplements that taste quite bad:** taurine, B vitamins, ozonated oil, vitamin C, shark cartilage, MSM.
- **Supplements that taste okay:** cysteine if dissolved in broth or grapefruit juice, pantothenate, ornithine, arginine, coenzyme Q10, potassium gluconate (salty), beta carotene, vitamin A, wintergreen, folic acid, Chinese herb (Yunnan Paiyao) biotin, niacin, betaine, calcium, magnesium.
- **Supplements that taste good:** inositol (sweetish), fennel, turmeric, moose elm.

More do's and don'ts about supplements:

- **Always wash a color-coated tablet under the kitchen faucet to remove the dye.**
- **Dunk in vitamin B_2 powder and set to dry on paper towel.**
- **Take coenzyme Q10 in the morning upon rising, before or after thyroid.**
- **Lugol's must be taken by itself with water at end of meals to avoid oxidizing your vitamins and food.**

Supplements can be mixed together, stirred into cereal, mashed potatoes, pudding, or rice and gulped down at beginning of meal.

Always keep bread nearby when taking supplements. If one should stick in your throat eat a bit of bread.

If nausea threatens, eat bits of bread, not liquid. Take two drops of mint oil.

If a stomachache threatens, sip hot water.

For spasms of intestine, sip hot water or take one niacinamide.

Don't take supplements at bedtime, especially B vitamins, because they are too energizing. But calcium and magnesium with hot moose elm are soporific.

Bloating and Gassiness

This is caused by food bacteria, *E. coli, Shigella, and Salmonella*. Take:

- **Turmeric six capsules, (one teaspoon), three times a day**
- **Fennel six capsules, (one teaspoon), three times a day.**

These herbs can be purchased in bulk. Mix with water and a little vinegar or water and a little honey to make a cocktail.

- **Lugol's iodine 6 drops (10 drops if bought) in ½ glass water taken after meals and bedtime. Not if allergic to iodine.**

If there is no relief in 24 hours, you are continuing to reinfect from food. Sterilize all food.

Intestinal Blockage or Bleeding

- **Moose elm (also called slippery elm), one to two tablespoons a day, made into "cocoa"**
- **Sodium alginate, two teaspoons powder a day added to one pint boiling water or simply blended in cold water**

These two can heal the intestinal wall where tumorous growths have caused bleeding, ulceration and pain. They may be combined with any food or each other. Use both.

Poor Digestion

- **Multiple digestive enzymes,** two to three with each meal. Helps food leave the stomach to relieve "full" feeling. Relieves heartburn and hiatal hernia.
- **Hydrochloric acid (5%),** 15 drops distributed in food and beverages at mealtime. Stir while adding. Never put drops straight in mouth because it dissolves tooth enamel! Check blood chloride levels after six weeks. Do not exceed 45 drops a day (not including cooking routines).

Better Digestion

Cancer patients have been parasitized in the liver. The liver is the seat of digestion. It controls appetite, too. Even though parasites are dead, and heavy metals, solvents and food dyes are gone, a weak digestion is still present. We must select food and a style of cooking that makes digestion easier.

Ascaris parasites block pepsin and acid secretion in the stomach. The stomach may have suffered for years in this way.

HEALTHY RECIPES

Although they are gone, we must still focus on food that is kind to the stomach. Taking pills at mealtime is certainly not soothing either. But raw beet juice helps in several ways, together with HCl drops and vinegar.

Raw Beet Cocktail

- **several medium size red beets**
- **HCl-water**
- **white vinegar**

Peel the beets before washing or rinsing them. Avoid getting dirt on the freshly cut surfaces. It does not wash off. Peel one half first. Then rinse one hand and hold the peeled half. Finish peeling. Drop into HCl-water to sterilize. Remove and cut in quarters. Add an equal volume of water to blend. "Liquefy" in blender for one minute or until smooth. Add half as much vinegar and blend again. Store in refrigerator. Serve 2 tbs. of beet cocktail just before each meal, adding 1 drop HCl. Light-treat.

Variations:

1. Add 1 tsp. sweetening per serving.
2. Add cysteine supplement (it is "covered" by beet flavor and sterilizes at the same time).

Beet Juice

Extracting the juice and discarding the pulp makes a stronger potion for anti-phenol (better digestion) action. If you have extreme pain or very bad digestion, choose beet juice as your cocktail. Peel, wash, and sterilize as before. After juicing add 1 tsp. vinegar per 2 oz. serving, and two drops HCl when served.

Variations: add fruit juice in small amounts; increase vinegar to suit taste; sweeten or spice in other ways.

Diarrhea and Constipation

Both are caused by the toxins produced by bacteria (the wrong bacteria) in the intestine. Killing them is the fastest way to relief.

Start with the anti-bacterial program: Lugol's (6 drops in ½ glass water). Ten minutes later turmeric (1 tsp. or 6 caps stirred into water), plus fennel (1 tsp. or 6 caps stirred into water). Later: 10 drops HCl (5%, USP) in a glass of water. Zap continuously for hours daily.

At the same time start taking sodium alginate (2 tsp. blended in 1 cup cold water). Sip it during the day.

Do not use anti-diarrhea drugs except as a last resort, since the bacterial problem will worsen while peristalsis is slowed.

If constipation continues, use Cascara Sagrada capsules (as directed). Also try Epsom salts (as directed on package). Also try *lactulose* available at pharmacies. Since you will be giving yourself an enema at bedtime, the constipation will do little harm.

Bowel Program

Bacteria are always at the root of bowel problems, such as pain, bloating and gassiness. They can not be killed by zapping, because the high frequency current does not penetrate the bowel contents.

Although most bowel bacteria are beneficial, the ones that are not, like *Salmonellas* and *Shigellas*, are extremely detrimental because they have the ability to invade the rest of your body and colonize a trauma site or weakened organ. These same bacteria colonize a cancer tumor and delay healing after the malignancy is stopped.

Another reason bowel bacteria are so hard to eradicate is that we are constantly reinfecting ourselves by keeping a reservoir on our hands and under our fingernails.

So the first thing to do is **improve sanitation**. For a serious problem, use 50% grain alcohol (100 proof vodka) in a spray bottle at the bathroom sink. Sterilize your hands after bathroom use and before meals.

Secondly use **turmeric** (2 capsules 3 times a day, this is the common spice) which I find helps against *Shigella*, as well as *E. coli*. Expect orange colored stool.

Third use **fennel** (1 capsule 3 times a day).

Fourth use **digestive enzyme tablets** with meals as directed on the bottle. (But only as long as necessary, because these frequently harbor molds.)

Fifth use a single 2 tsp. dose of **Black Walnut Hull Tincture Extra Strength**. Add it to a ½ glass of water and sip over a 15-minute period. Stay seated until any side effect from the alcohol wears off.

Sixth take **Cascara Sagrada** capsules if constipated (start with one capsule a day, use up to maximum on label). Remember to drink a cup of hot water upon rising in the morning. This will begin to regulate your elimination.

It can take all six to get rid of a bad *Shigella* problem in a week. Afterward, you must continue to eat only sterile dairy products. Note that the *Kidney Cleanse* is often effective with bowel problems. Try it also.

You will know you succeeded when your tummy is flat, there is not a single gurgle, and your mood improves!

Anemia

"Building" blood can be the single most important task for you.

Iron is necessary for your body in many ways, besides making hemoglobin for your red blood cells. Muscle activity depends on myoglobin—much like hemoglobin; it contains iron.

Iron must not be in competition with copper, either. Copper water pipes and copper seeping from metal or plastic dentalware or from killed fungus keep blood iron levels too low.

With parasites and other toxins gone, the iron level promptly rises and may reach forty from a value below 35 in the first five days, getting to a more normal level of 50 to 60 in three weeks.

The low iron level in cancer has been known a very long time and is referred to as "anemia of chronic disease," which includes "anemia of malignancy." It is, more accurately, "anemia from *Ascaris*, copper, lanthanide and asbestos toxicity." It is the unavailability of iron in the midst of plenty (of ferric iron) that strangles the cancer patient's metabolism and ultimately causes fatality in roughly half the failing cases I see, not the tumors themselves. Fortunately when you kill Ascaris and take iron, this anemia clears up.

Insomnia

All insomnia I have seen is due to bacteria in the brain. The supplements given here do not correct the problem (only killing bacteria at their source does), they only give relief. Make sure you are correcting the problem at the same time as getting relief. Do not take vitamins or supplements at bedtime (except Lugol's, calcium, magnesium) because they tend to energize you. A hot shower is helpful, too, as is chamomile tea.

- **Ornithine 500 mg, take six or eight for a strong effect.**
- **Melatonin 2 mg, take two for a strong effect.**

They may be taken together.

Lymphoma

In the lymphomas, butyrates are absent in the lymph nodes. They represent the oil of butter. They are present in healthy people. It is known that the enzyme, tributyrinase, is very low (10%) after feeding the azo dye DAB. This could account for low levels of butyrate. The Syncrometer® detects the absence of butyrates in the lymph nodes if toxic germanium is present or isopropyl compounds (isopropylidene nucleic acids) are present. This suggests that the absence of good germanium allows isopropyl-caused mutations to occur preferentially at a butyrate-related gene such as the tributyrinase enzyme. Giving a supplement of butyrate to lymphoma patients was already advanced in 1982. The dose is 3 gm daily.

Liver Cancer

These are commonly used by alternative cancer doctors. Try some or all or milk thistle powder, 2 heaping tsp. daily.
- **Silymarin** (milk thistle concentrate), take 2 three times a day.
- **Cesium chloride** 3 to 6 gm a day after meals (provided clinically only). May give side effects like nausea. Intended to push excess sodium out of cells to rehabilitate them.
- **Urea powder** (provided clinically only), 3 to 6 tsp. a day, dissolved in beverages.
- **Raw beef liver juice** sterilized with hydrochloric acid, 1 oz. daily.
- **Raw bitters** (foraged greens), sterilized with hydrochloric acid. Use raw peeled aloe vera if other herbs not available.
- **Glycyrrhizin** (licorice extract), 2 capsules three times a day.

Bone Cancer

To heal bone, you need calcium, magnesium, and bone hardeners: manganese and boron.

Calcium carbonate, 500 mg, take one a day. Do not take calcium if blood test shows calcium level is over 9.6. Take with meals. Capsules are preferred, so you can dissolve more of it. Be sure your brand is lead-free. (Ask for a lead analysis.)

Magnesium oxide, 300 mg, take one 3 times a day at beginning of meals. Capsules are preferred.

Boron, 1 mg, take one with each meal, twice as much if in pain.

Manganese, 10 mg, take one a day for one month. Then stop.

By prescription *Clodronate* (or equivalent), two tablets, three times a day. This is sodium diphosphonate; it stops further dissolving of bones.

Vitamin D, 25,000 IU per day for 10 days, then 25,000 IU twice a week only. Do not use vitamin D if blood test shows calcium level is over 9.6. Vitamin D is a differentiator, meaning it causes cells to return to their normal work. It causes inositol phosphate to appear in tumor cells and remove calcium deposits so the digestion-flag can be raised. Excess (over 50,000 IU per day) is toxic!

Kill Bacteria

With the immune system down, a cancer patient is as helpless as an infant in a burning building. So food and fingers must be sterilized before eating. Use these five systems to kill the truly harmful parasites and bacteria.

Lugol's iodine. This is curative for *Salmonella* infection, the most common cause of stomach discomfort or bloating. Do not take if allergic to iodine. Also use Lugol's as mouthwash, hand wash and general disinfectant, diluting 1 drop in a cup of water.

Colloidal silver, homemade. Six drops on tooth brush after meals. One tablespoon as mouthwash, gargle. Swallow. Is particularly effective against *Clostridium*. Use one to four tbs. for pain, up to ½ cup in acute situations.

Oregano oil, of the variety *Oreganum vulgare* specifically kills *Clostridium*. To penetrate a tumor, though, you must use 20 drops three times a day for several days. To avoid burning your tongue, put them in an empty capsule and swallow. Any drops on the outside should be washed off. You may have bread and a beverage with it.

Cysteine. $1/8$ teaspoon per quart clear liquid kills parasites and bacteria. Use twice as much if liquid has particulate matter.

This will not kill *Toxoplasma* or *Leishmania*, which are also found in plain dirt. To kill these an equal amount of salt must be added. Cysteine and salt is particularly compatible with buttermilk, yogurt, blended cottage cheese, and eggs. One tsp. cysteine (4000 mg) by mouth kills many parasites and bacteria internally; consume within ½ hour, may cause temporary side effects at this dosage. Eat solid food afterward to reduce side effects.

Hydrochloric acid (HCl 5%), 3 drops in a glass of water three times a day kills bacteria in the stomach, but also reaches the gall bladder to help the liver kill its bacteria. <u>Do not take straight in mouth—it dissolves teeth</u>.

Kill Leftover Pathogens

Betaine hydrochloride. This is the only supplement we know that can clear the intestinal tract of Clostridium bacteria; therefore it is essential to your recovery. Betaine will <u>not</u> clear Clostridium from your teeth. It is also a methyl group supplier.

Ozonated oil can distribute itself to locations where ozone as a gas or ozonated water cannot reach. It can detoxify benzene in the body (changing it to phenol) similar to the action of vitamin B_2. We have seen it kill various bacteria and viruses when monitoring with the Syncrometer®. Even *Leishmania* and malaria parasites have disappeared after several weeks' use but more research is needed to confirm this, and also to establish a mechanism of its action, as well as a level of safety.

I have found that it does not oxidize vitamin C into breakdown products in the body. But it <u>does</u> oxidize some vitamin E. For this reason a supplement of vitamin E should be taken 5 hours <u>after</u> taking ozonated oil. If it is taken sooner than this, the ozonated oil is neutralized before it has completed its action. Until more is known, caution is advised; use only with the mop-up program and liver cleanse (<u>not as an ongoing supplement</u>).

It must be sterilized, preferably before ozonating (2 drops HCl per cup, shaken), since most oils on the market are contaminated with *Ascaris* eggs and larvae.

Inositol is a sugar-like compound with unique features. It is ultra-oxidized, having six molecules of oxygen attached to it. It is missing in organs that are infected with bacteria. When inositol is eaten it is transformed into two new molecules. The Syncrometer® now detects rhodizonic acid and L-ascorbic acid!

Could eating inositol regularly provide this "mystery oxidizer" that seems to be lacking in adults, just as Dr. Koch imagined? And would it keep us deparasitized and detoxified automatically?

It is also baffling in a second, more obvious way. We have been taught that humans cannot make their own ascorbic acid. Yet here we see it appear from a precursor compound. It is as if internal oxidation-reduction occurred in the inositol molecule, producing rhodizonic acid, an oxidizer and ascorbic acid, a reducer. More research is needed to confirm this.

Inositol Phosphate is formed after six phosphate molecules have combined with inositol, one at each OH. This makes the new molecule (popularly called IP6) quite acid and able to combine with the calcium deposits created by lanthanides. Remember, calcium deposits prevent the digestion flag to appear. Tumor cells do not have IP6, although others do. Although removing lanthanides is most important, we can speed up removal of calcium deposits by giving IP6, also called phytic acid. Take 10 drops of a 50% solution, three times a day, in ½ cup plain water before meals or water with inositol added.

Wintergreen oil (natural only, not distilled or synthetic) is another mysterious helper that needs more research. I believe it seeks out tumors, turning them into cysts with liquid centers, as seen on a scan. Take three drops, three times a day (excess is toxic). It is also a traditional tumor shrinker.

Kill Adenovirus

(common cold)

- **eucalyptus, 2 X 2**
- **Reishi mushroom, 1 X 2**
- **epazote, 2 X 2**
- **boneset, 2 X 2**
- **elecampane, 2 X 2**
- **cleavers, 2 X 2**
- **2 tsp. lipase to remove all oils, once a day**
- **pancreatin-lipase, 2 X 4**

Oscillococcinum is just as useful to prevent colds as the flu. (The eucalyptus, Reishi mushroom, epazote and boneset can be made into teas. Just drop the capsule into hot water and sweeten with Agave syrup.)

Herbal Treatment of Whooping Cough

At the first signs of a cold or slight cough, make a tea using the following:

- **½ part sundew**
- **1 part coltsfoot**
- **1 part elecampane**
- **1 part squills**
- **1 part thyme**

Sweeten with licorice, and add honey if necessary. Give the tea as often as you can, up to the equivalent of four to six cups a day.

If treated properly when it first starts, the symptoms should not worsen to the "whooping" stage. If you miss the first stage and the "whoop" sets in, you can still use the same recipe, giving tea every hour or so, and add one or two of the following herbs: wild cherry bark, wild lettuce, red clover.

Teas may be taken as often as possible, sweetened with licorice, honey or aniseed.

Tinctures are easier because they are concentrated. Between five and ten drops of the mixture can be given in a drink every two hours; or every hour if the condition is serious.

Utilize hand and foot baths using teas or tinctures, diluted in water, two to four times daily.

To use essential oils choose from basil, cypress, marjoram or thyme, use them in vaporizers, in massage oils for the chest, feet or abdomen. A few drops can be put on the pillow at night, or used in a plant spray bottle to spray the room.

Kill Tapeworms

- **Sage**
- **Thyme**
- **Anise**
- **Coriander**
- **Caraway Seed**
- **Fennel**
- **Allspice**
- **Juniper**
- **Nutmeg**

Put two (2) drops of each oil into an empty capsule. Take immediately. Take twice daily for three (3) days.

For people over 200 lbs. use three (3) drops of each oil three (3) times daily for three (3) days.

Restore Major Minerals

Calcium. There is a serious deficit of calcium in all cancer patients even when tumors themselves have too much and blood levels are much too high! But we cannot give more while blood levels are too high, called hypercalcemia. The problem in this case is in the thyroid gland. As soon as the thyroid problem, itself due to toxins and bacteria from teeth, is corrected, the calcium level may plummet, revealing the true shortage.

Magnesium (oxide) should be taken as a powder, like calcium, to help it dissolve in the stomach. Taken as a powder, it does not cause diarrhea. It is a major enzyme activator. There is a severe deficit in cancer patients. Magnesium helps to detoxify phenol. Phenol is produced by *Streptococcus* bacteria, and also comes from benzene. Phenol is even produced during digestion by the liver. High doses of magnesium are needed during the time when benzene, dyes, and plasticizers are being mobilized from the body tissues and newly opened tumors. After this, a lower dose may be taken. Take at the <u>beginning</u> of meals. Magnesium also reduces anxiety, relieves pain, protects the heart, and stops spasms of many kinds.

Potassium gluconate. There is a severe deficiency of potassium in the tissues of a cancer patient. Even ½ teaspoon of potassium gluconate powder, which contains 240 mg potassium, taken three times a day does not bring up the level to its correct value for several weeks. The level should be 4.6 or 4.7; <u>but no higher</u>. For this reason, you should not exceed ½ teaspoon three times a day, and <u>must</u> monitor your blood at least every three weeks.

Potassium is a respiration stimulant, causing increased uptake of oxygen, exactly what is wanted to restore health to the tumorous organ. After a blood level of 4.7 is reached, <u>stop</u>. Never take potassium gluconate for more than 3 weeks without getting a new blood test.

> ALWAYS use a <u>measuring</u> spoon to portion out powdered supplements. To find the equivalent dose in capsules, empty them into a measuring spoon and record the number used.

Get The Ammonia Out

Ornithine and Arginine. When an organ is besieged by bacteria it is overwhelmed by the ammonia they make. Ammonia is the same fume that comes from a diaper pail. Our livers can detoxify it very quickly, but not other organs because they can't do the chemistry called the *urea synthesis cycle*. Other organs must ship any ammonia made in them to the liver.

In the urea synthesis cycle two molecules of ammonia are pinned together with a carbon dioxide molecule to make a single urea molecule. Urea is odorless, tasteless, and harmless. Urea can be excreted easily into the bladder, but it is useful in several ways before it is excreted. It helps to keep the osmotic strength of the blood up so liquid cannot seep out and cause edema. Urea in pure crystalline form (28 grams in a liter of water in one day) is often given by mouth to cancer patients in alternative treatment centers, especially for liver cancer (provided the blood level of BUN is not already too high). It is well tolerated and does not raise the BUN for several weeks, after which it can be stopped.

Ornithine and arginine both play a role in the urea synthesis cycle probably expanding it and speeding it up and thereby helping the liver detoxify the whole body from ammonia. It is like supplying more trucks and wagons to do a hauling job. Removing ammonia returns each cell to a less alkaline state, giving strength to the cells' own ability to kill bacteria (lysosomes must keep themselves acidic). Arginine is particularly beneficial in combating Clostridium bacteria. But it takes a lot of arginine to keep up with the ammonia production of a moderate Clostridium infection. Three tablespoons was needed at first to control *Clostridium* in tumors. After finding the real source of *Clostridium* (Rabbit fluke and tooth microleakage) and getting rid of them, we could reduce the dose to one sixth of that!

There may be an actual shortage of ornithine and arginine in the tumorous tissue because these amino acids are consumed in the manufacture of *polyamines*. During cell division large quantities of *diamines* and polyamines are made to somehow satisfy the needs of chromosomes. The enzymes, arginase and ornithine decarboxylase, makers of these polyamines, are always working overtime (remember that cobalt stimulates arginase) in cancer patients and using up arginine and ornithine. This way a shortage of arginine and ornithine could easily develop and stall the urea synthesis cycle. This would worsen the ammonia buildup, ruin cells' immunity, and allow a runaway *Clostridium* infection.

When you begin to feel sleepy by daytime, the ornithine dose can be reduced but not the arginine dose.

Supply Amino Acids

Essential and Nonessential Amino Acids. Amino acids are the building blocks for protein. Essential amino acids are the ones that the body can't make. Non-essential are the ones that it can (when the person is healthy). But cancer patients have a considerable handicap in interconverting (making) amino acids. Often none or just a few are detected in the tumorous organ. This could also be due to lack of ATP energy to operate the transport mechanisms that pull them into the cells. To heal, cells must have amino acids; they cannot wait for health to improve first. So don't be deceived, even the "non-essential" ones are essential.

There are 19 ingredients altogether. It takes large doses before they are detectable by Syncrometer®. And they will not stay present unless taken daily for a few weeks.

Instead of chicken broth, use the broth of Rock Cornish hen or turkey. All chicken samples we tested carried the c-MYC oncogene as well as another virus that we dubbed.

Raw Chicken Virus tested carried both of these. Rock Cornish hen and turkey did not carry them. Cooking did not kill them. Cooking plus 10 minutes full-spectrum light DID kill them. It seems much too risky to eat chicken.

It is, of course, not the fault of chickens. They would prefer to be well too. Their feed, if made of animal refuse, could bring them these oncogenic viruses.

Both shark cartilage and chicken broth help cells replenish their amino acids in days, not weeks; perhaps this is due to the RNAse inhibitor they contain.

Shark Cartilage helps replenish RNAse inhibitor and amino acids as well as providing other factors. But it must be sterilized with cysteine-salt water ($^1/_{16}$ teaspoon each per cup liquid) or by adding HCl drops. Not many brands have RNAse inhibitor present. It must be a casualty of processing. For this reason we always add chicken broth to the cancer program besides shark cartilage.

Glutamic acid is a very versatile amino acid and can be transformed into other amino acids. By picking up ammonia it changes to glutamine, which has further uses. One use is making purines, which in turn makes uric acid. So when your blood uric acid level is low it indicates a need for glutamic acid. I recommend taking glutamic acid separately from the "mix" because so much more is needed. A large dose, 1 tbs. three times a day, often brings a sense of well being immediately.

Glycine is the simplest of all amino acids and for this reason can be made from others, and it should therefore never be low according to classical textbooks. But I find cancer patients don't have it! Glycine is used to make creatine, which in turn makes creatinine. So when your blood creatinine is low, I believe there is a shortage of glycine. In addition to the "mix," take ½ tsp. three times a day if creatinine levels are below 0.8.

Return Immunity

Papain and bromelain are plant enzymes often used to help digestion. I use them because they can digest the ferritin off white blood cells (at least papain has been studied in this regard, bromelain was discovered by Syncrometer®). Previously when we discussed ferritin, it was the hero that sacrificed itself to surround the villain asbestos. Why are we now trying to digest it? Because there is a drawback to using ferritin. Ferritin, as it coats and smears the outside surface of white blood cells, inadvertently "blinds" them. Their surface has the receptors, which sense enemy molecules, acting as their "eyes and ears." Digesting ferritin lets the white blood cells regain their "sight." They can now find other white blood cells to pass their toxic cargo to, which is the normal method.

Now tissues can be cleared of asbestos much more quickly. And excess damaged ferritin is no longer present, exposing its ferric iron, which was oxidizing good germanium. Immunity has returned.

We give 1 tsp. papain twice a day in a beverage before meals. (Be careful not to inhale it, you could start an allergic reaction.) Bromelain is much more palatable, though less effective. You can use 1 tsp. (4000 mg) two times a day instead of papain. But in serious illness use both.

Selenium can be detected by the Syncrometer® as sodium sele<u>nite</u> in healthy organs, never as sele<u>nate</u> (so I assume that is the beneficial form). But in the presence of ferritin coated white blood cells or phenol or Ascaris produced chemicals, only the selenate form is detected. It switches back to selenite as soon as the above abnormal oxidizers are gone. Lack of selenite stalls the unloading from White Blood Cells. They seem to be bursting with high bacteria and toxin levels soon after ferritin and lanthanides are gone, yet unable to dispatch and unload these until large amounts of selenite are consumed. It typically requires 3,000 to 4,000 mcg daily for 3 weeks. Fresh coconut is a good source after that, when much smaller amounts are needed. Selenite can be detected now when one half coconut is eaten for three days straight. If raw coconut is not available, continue taking sodium selenite, but at a reduced level, 1000 mcg a day, for several months after all tumors are gone.

Bring Back Iron

Methyl sulfonyl methane (MSM) is a powerful substance that can return your ferric iron and bad germanium to ferrous iron and good germanium! Even while asbestos is still present and ferritin has coated the white blood cells! Use ½ tsp. twice a day for 3 weeks; double this dose if severely ill. This will not remove asbestos or dyes.

Remove Calcium Deposits

Vitamin D can induce inositol phosphates IP6, IP2 and IP3 to appear in the correct ratios even when none were there before. This results in the disappearance of calcium deposits much faster than if using only the magnet. A hard bony tumor may begin to soften in a few days. Use 25,000 units of cholecalciferol daily for 21 days. No more. It can be toxic. Use only if calcium levels are below 9.7. Vitamin D is a known differentiator, causing cells to "get to work" making the right proteins.

Digest the Tumor

Enzymes, including pancreatin, lipase, DNAse, peroxidase, and catalase are produced by the body in large amounts. The Syncrometer® detects all these in every organ; but not in the tumor or its white blood cells.

We have been taught that digestive enzymes stay in the digestive tract. And that eating them would do no good since they would be themselves digested. This may be partly true, but only partly. The tumor can be deluged with pancreatin and lipase by taking 1 tsp. of each between meals 3 times a day. "Enzyme therapy" was discovered long ago by cancer therapists and was built into several alternative programs. But will the flood of enzymes digest the tumor? Only if lanthanides and the calcium deposits they cause are gone, so the cell "flag" may be raised, saying "I am ready for digestion…come and get me." The flag, phosphatidyl serine appears on the cell surface when calcium deposits, particularly calcium triphosphate, are gone. At this point the enzymes are exceedingly swift. In one week a large bite can be missing from the tumor.

We use horseradish sauce (Heinz brand) to supply peroxidase and catalase since the dried herb is missing catalase. Use three tsp. daily on food.

Healthy Helpers

Natural Body Product Recipes

You can use just borax (like 20 Mule Team Borax™) for all types of cleaning including your body, laundry, dishes and your house! You don't need all those products you see in commercials for each special task!

Even if you have dry skin, difficult hair or some other unique requirement, just pure borax will satisfy these needs. A part of every skin problem is due to the toxic elements found in the soaps themselves. For instance aluminum is commonly added as a "skin moisturizer". It does this by impregnating the skin and attracting water, giving the illusion of moist skin. In fact you simply have <u>moist aluminum</u> stuck in your skin, which your immune system must remove. While borax won't directly heal your skin or complexion, it does replace the agents that are causing damage, so that healing can occur.

Borax Liquid Soap

- **An empty 1 gallon jug**
- **$1/8$ cup borax powder**
- **Plastic funnel**

Funnel the borax into the jug, fill with <u>hot</u> tap water. Shake a few times. Let settle. In a few minutes you can pour off the clear part into dispenser bottles. This is the soap!

Easier way: use any bottle; pour borax powder to a depth of a ½ inch or so. Add water. Shake. When you have used it down to the undissolved granules, discard them and start over.

Keep a dispenser of borax soap by the kitchen sink, bathroom sink, and shower. It does not contain aluminum as regular detergents and soaps do, and which contribute to Alzheimer's disease. It does not contain PCBs as many commercial and health food varieties do. It does not contain cobalt (the blue or green granules), which causes heart disease and poisons the bone marrow. Commercial detergents and non-soaps are simply not safe. Switch to homemade bar soap and borax for all your tasks! In fact, you could add a tbs. of homemade liquid soap to the borax to make it sudsy. Borax inhibits the bacterial enzyme *urease* and is therefore anti-bacterial. It may even clear your skin of blemishes and stop your scalp from itching.

Laundry

Borax (½-cup per load). It is the main ingredient of non-chlorine bleach and has excellent cleaning power without fading colors. It can be combined with homemade soap for extra cleaning power. Your regular laundry soap may contain PCBs, aluminum, cobalt and other chemicals. These get rubbed into your skin constantly as you wear your clothing. For bleaching (only do this occasionally) use original chlorine bleach (not "new improved" or "with special brighteners", and so forth). Don't use chlorine if there is an ill person in the house. For getting out stubborn dirt at collars, rub in homemade bar soap first; for stains, try grain alcohol, vinegar, baking soda (check old recipe books for stain removal tricks).

Dishes

Don't believe your eyes when you see the commercials where the smiling person pulls a shining dish out of greasy suds. Any dish soap that you use should be safe enough to eat because nothing rinses off clean. Regular dish detergents, including health brands, are now polluted with PCBs. They also contain harmful chemicals like cobalt. Use borax for your dishes. Or use paper plates and plastic (not styrofoam) cups.

Dishwasher

Use 2 tsp. borax powder straight or pre-dissolved in water. If you use too much it will leave a film on your dishes. Use vinegar in the rinse cycle to reduce film.

Sink

Use a dishpan in the sink. Use ¼ cup borax and add a minimum of water. Also keep a bit of dry borax in a saucer by the sink for scouring. Don't use any soap at all for dishes that aren't greasy and can be washed under the faucet with nothing but running water. Throw away your old sponge or brush or cloth because it may be PCB contaminated. Start each day by sterilizing your sponge (it harbors Salmonella) or with a new one while the used one dries for three full days. Clean greasy pots and pans with a paper towel first. Then use homemade bar soap.

Shampoo

Borax liquid is ready to use as shampoo, too. It does not lather but feels slippery between your fingers (If it is not slippery, the concentration is too low. Check the recipe). It goes right to work removing sweat and soil without stripping your color or natural oils. It inhibits scalp bacteria and stops flaking and itching. Hair gets squeaky clean so quickly (just a few squirts does it) that you might think nothing has happened! You will soon be accustomed to non-lathery soap. Rinse very thoroughly because you should leave your scalp slightly acidic.

Take a pint container to the shower with you for rinsing. Put ¼ tsp. <u>citric</u> (not ascorbic) acid crystals in it. For long hair use a quart of rinse. Only **citric acid** is strong enough to rinse the borax out, lemon juice and vinegar are <u>not</u>. After shampooing, fill the rinse container with water and pour over your head. Your hair should feel instantly silky. Rinse your whole body, too, since citric acid is also anti-bacterial. All hair shampoo penetrates the eyelids and gets into the eyes although you do not feel it. It is important to use this natural rinse to neutralize the shampoo in your eyes. (Some people have stated that citric acid makes their hair curlier or reddens it. If this is undesirable, use only half as much citric acid.) Citric acid also conditions and gives body and sheen to hair. A single squirt of homemade liquid soap added to borax liquid makes it quite lathery if you need time to adjust to plain borax.

Baking Soda Shampoo

- 1 tbs. baking soda
- 1 cup very hot water

Place both in a plastic container and stir with your fingers until dissolved. Scoop it up over your hair by hand; if you pour it, too much runs off.

Hair Spray

I don't have a recipe that holds your hair as well as the bottle of chemicals you can buy at the store. Remarkably, a little lemon juice (not from a bottle) has some holding power and no odor! Buy a 1-cup spray bottle, squeeze part of a lemon, letting only the clear juice run into the bottle. Fill with water. Keep in the refrigerator. Make fresh every week. Spraying with just plain water is nearly as good! For shinier hair, drop a bit of lemon peel into the bottle.

Homemade Soap

- **A small plastic dishpan, about 10" x 12"**
- **A glass or enamel 2-quart sauce pan**
- **1 can of lye (sodium hydroxide), 12 ounces**
- **3 pounds of lard (BHT and BHA are OK here)**
- **Plastic gloves**
- **Water**

1. Pour 3 cups of very cold water (refrigerate water overnight first) into the 2-quart saucepan.

2. Slowly and carefully add the lye, a little bit at a time, stirring it with a wooden or plastic utensil. (Use plastic gloves for this; test them for holes first.) Do not breathe the vapor or lean over the container or have children nearby. Above all <u>use no metal</u>. The mixture will get very hot. In olden days, a sassafras branch was used to stir, imparting a fragrance and insect deterrent for mosquitoes, lice, fleas, ticks.

3. Let cool at least one hour in a safe place. Meanwhile, the unwrapped lard should be warming up to room temperature in the plastic dishpan.

4. Slowly and carefully, pour the lye solution into the dishpan with the lard. The lard will melt. Mix thoroughly, at least 15 minutes, until it looks like thick pudding.

5. Let it set until the next morning; then cut it into bars. It will get harder after a few days. Then package.

If you wish to make soap based on olive oil, use about 48 ounces. It may need to harden for a week.

Liquid Soap

Make chips from your homemade soap cake. Add enough hot water to dissolve. Add citric acid to balance the pH (7 to 8). If you do not, this soap may be too harsh for your skin, while it is excellent for cleaning the sink.

Skin Sanitizer

Make a 5 to 10% solution of food grade alcohol. Food grade alcohols are grain or cane (ethyl) alcohol. Only the large size Everclear bottle (750 ml or 1 liter) is free of isopropyl or wood alcohol contaminants. Purchase at a liquor store. Find a suitable dispenser bottle, mark with a pen about one tenth of the way up from the bottom. Pour 95% grain alcohol (190 proof) to this mark and add water to the top. If using 76% grain alcohol, mark your bottle one tenth of the way up but only add water to the ¾ full mark. Keep shut. Add a chip of lemon peel for fragrance.

Use this for general sanitizing purposes: bathroom fixtures, knobs, handles, canes, walkers, and for personal cleanliness (but use chlorine bleach for the toilet bowl once a week). Always clean up after a bowel movement with <u>wet</u> toilet paper. This is not clean enough, though. Follow with a stronger damp paper towel. This is still not clean enough; use a final damp paper towel with skin sanitizer added. After washing hands, sanitize them too, pouring a bit on one palm and put finger tips of the other hand in it, scratch to get under nails, repeat on other hand. Rinse with water. Remember to keep the toilet lid down, while flushing or a spray of *E. coli* will fill the bathroom air, settling on toothbrushes and in water glasses.

Wash your hands if you merely <u>touch</u> the toilet seat.

Deodorant

Your sweat is odorless. It is the entrenched bacteria feeding on it that make smells. You can never completely rid yourself of these bacteria, although they may temporarily be gone 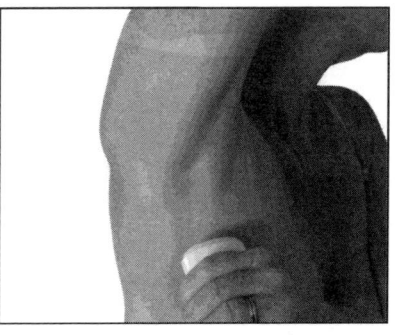 after zapping. The strategy is to control their numbers. Here are several deodorants to try. Find one that works best for you:

Vitamin C water. Mix ¼ tsp. to a pint of water and dab it on.

Citric Acid water. Mix ¼ tsp. to a pint of water and dab it on.

Only a few drops of these acids under each armpit are necessary. If these acids burn the skin, dilute them more. Never apply anything to skin that has just been shaved!

Lemon juice. This acid is not as strong, use what you need.

Cornstarch. Many people need only this. Dab it on.

Baking soda has been deleted as a deodorant because benzene was found in many boxes.

Pure alcohol (never rubbing alcohol). The only food grade alcohol is grain or cane (ethyl) alcohol. Dab a bit under each arm and/or on your shirt or blouse. If the alcohol burns, dilute it with water. Be very careful not to leave the bottle where a child or alcoholic person could find it. Pour it into a different bottle!

Pure zinc oxide. You may ask your pharmacist to order this for you. She or he may wish to make it up for you too, but do not let them add anything else to it. It should be about 1 part zinc oxide powder to 3 parts water. It does not dissolve. Just shake it up to use it. After you get it home, you can add cornstarch to it to give it a creamy texture. Heat 3 tsp. cornstarch in 1 cup of water, to boiling, until dissolved and clear. Cool and add some to the zinc oxide mixture (about equal parts). Store unused starch mixture in the refrigerator. Only make up enough for a month. (Yes, this is the same zinc oxide that is used to make the dental cement, ZOE.)

Alcohol and zinc oxide. This is the most powerful deodorant. Apply alcohol first, then the zinc oxide.

Remember that you need to sweat! Sweating excretes toxic substances, especially from the upper body. Don't use deodorant on weekends. Go to the sink and wipe clean the armpits like our grandparents did. These homemade deodorants are not as powerful as the commercial varieties—this is to your advantage.

Brushing Teeth

Buy a new toothbrush. Your old one is soaked with toxins from your old toothpaste. Use food-grade hydrogen peroxide if you have only plastic fillings. Dilute it from 35% to 17½% by adding water (equal parts). Store hydrogen peroxide only in polyethylene or the original plastic bottle. Use 4 or 5 drops on your toothbrush. It should fizz nicely as oxygen is produced in your mouth. Your teeth will whiten noticeably in six months.

Before brushing teeth, floss with monofilament fish line (2 or 4 pound). Double it and twist for extra strength. Rinse before use. Or clean up the commercial varieties of floss by soaking in water for a half hour, then drying with a towel. Do not choose waxed or flavored varieties since benzene does not wash off.

Floss and brush only once a day because even this small trauma invites bacteria and fungus into your blood. If this leaves you uncomfortable, you may use a water pick or simply rub your teeth by hand with a dry cloth towel (paper towels have mercury contamination). Make sure that nothing solid, like powder, is on your toothbrush; it will scour and scratch the enamel. Salt is corrosive—don't use it for brushing metal teeth. Plain water is just as good.

Baking soda is <u>no longer recommended</u> (unless ordered from *Sources*) because it was found to be polluted with benzene.

When battling tooth infection, alternate colloidal silver and white iodine solutions (five drops on brush), and brush twice a day.

Oregano Oil Toothpowder

- **10 tsp. baking soda disinfected by freezing**
- **10 drops oregano oil disinfected by freezing**

Be sure these ingredients are chlorox-free.

Place ingredients in zippered plastic bag. Squish the mixture in the bag till well mixed. Store in HDPE closed jar or keep in original bag. Freeze again to sanitize later. This is about a 2-month supply. Brushing daily will keep Clostridium bacteria at undetectable levels. Dip dry toothbrush in powder. But be careful, oregano oil straight in your mouth could make you jump with burning sensation although it does not harm you. If you accidentally get too much, chew bread and keep your tongue at the roof of your mouth.

Immediately after dental work your mouth is too sore to brush your teeth. In fact, it is unwise to use a brush at this time. Simply **rub** your teeth after flossing. Wind a strip of paper towel around your finger. Dampen with a few drops of water and dip into the powder.

Variations: Essential oils are too strong to be used daily, unless they are of the culinary variety. You may use 1 drop clove, ginger, basil, cardamom, peppermint, fennel, sage oil, but only once a day to avoid allergy.

Straight Dental Bleach is 4 times stronger than the mouthwash variety. It is .2% sodium hypochlorite. Use it to sterilize your dentures overnight.

Denture Cleaner

To keep your denture free of bacteria, disinfect it every night, rotating the disinfectant. Also use salt water. It kills all germs and is inexpensive. Salt water plus grain alcohol or food-grade hydrogen peroxide makes a good denture-soak. Rinse well.

- Dentures that acquire gray or fine-lined discoloration are growing Clostridium bacteria! Kill them by brushing with *straight Dental Bleach*. Let denture stand without rinsing until the discoloration is gone. Rinse with vitamin C water (add ½ capsule vitamin C to ½ cup water). Rotate the following treatments:
- Soak in *straight Dental Bleach* overnight once a week. This is 0.2% sodium hypochlorite (NSF grade). Rinse with vitamin C water. If you use it more often you could get allergic to chlorine! BEWARE.
- **Sonicate once a week in a small jewelry cleaner.**
- **Ozonate twice a week.**
- **Soak in salt water, ¼ tsp. pure salt to ¼ cup water three times a week.**

Alcohol, Lugol's and weak salt solution are not strong enough. Commercial solutions have dyes, sweetener and must be tested.

Don't keep partials or dentures in your mouth at night. Your mouth should <u>always</u> smell sweet.

Denture Adhesive

- **1 rounded tsp. sodium alginate**
- **1 cup water**
- **2 tsp. grain alcohol (Everclear only), this is only for preservation, not essential.**

Let mixture stand in water 4 or more hours till completely dissolved. To make it stronger, add more alginate and wait longer. Keep notes on your favorite concentration. Don't use commercial sources that are colored blue or green. The coloring is due to methylene blue dye or a cobalt compound.

This powder can be used straight, dusted lightly on denture after wetting denture surface. Use plastic salt shaker.

Mouthwash

A few drops of food grade hydrogen peroxide added to a little water in a glass should be enough to make your mouth foam and cleanse. Don't use hydrogen peroxide, though, if you have metal fillings, because they react. Don't use regular drug store variety hydrogen peroxide because it contains toxic additives. Health food store varieties contain solvents from the bottling process. Never purchase hydrogen peroxide in a bottle with a metal cap.

For persons with metal tooth fillings just use plain hot water. A healthy mouth has no odor! You shouldn't need a mouthwash! If you have breath odor, it is probably *Clostridium* growing in the crevice between a tooth filling and the tooth. At least, search for a hidden tooth infection by getting a panoramic x-ray and visiting your dentist.

Contact Lens Solution

A scant cup of cold tap water brought to a boil in glass saucepan. After adding ¼ tsp. pure salt and boiling again, pour into a sterile canning jar. Refrigerate. Freeze some of it.

Lip Soother

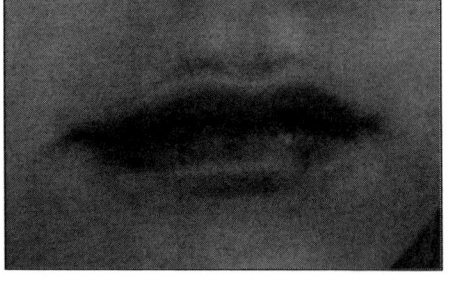

For dry, burning lips, heat 1 level tsp. sodium alginate, plus 1-cup water until dissolved. Cool, pour it into a small bottle to carry in your purse or pocket (refrigerate the remainder). Dab it on whenever needed. If the consistency isn't right for you, add water or boil it down further. You can make a better lip soother by adding some lysine from a crushed tablet, vitamin C powder, and a vitamin E capsule to the alginate mix. If you have a persistent problem with chapped lips, try going off citrus juice.

Foot Powder

Use a mixture of cornstarch and zinc oxide poured into a tall saltshaker with large holes in the lid. Add long rice grains to fight humidity. You may also try arrowroot or potato starch. If you don't have zinc oxide use plain cornstarch.

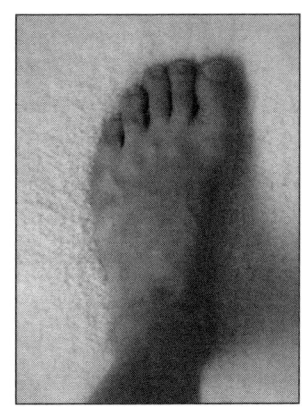

Skin Healer Moisturizer Lotion

- 1 tsp. sodium alginate
- 1 cup water

Make the base first by heating these together in a covered, non-metal pan until completely dissolved. Use low heat–it will take over an hour. Use a wooden spoon handle to stir. Set aside. Then make the following mixture:
- ¼ tsp. vitamin C (ascorbic acid)
- ¼ tsp. lysine
- 2 tbs. pure vegetable glycerin
- 2 vitamin E capsules (400 units or more, each)
- 1 tsp. olive oil
- 1 tbs. lemon juice from a lemon or ¼ tsp. citric acid (this is optional)
- 1 cup water

Heat the water to steaming in a non-metal pan. Add vitamin C and lysine first and then everything else. Pour into a pint jar and shake to mix. Then add the sodium alginate base to the desired thickness (about equal amounts) and shake. Pour some into a small bottle to use as lip soother. Pour some into a larger bottle to dispense on skin; store remainder in refrigerator. Sodium alginate is also available in capsule form at some health food stores.)

Other Skin Healers

Vitamin C powder (ascorbic acid, not the same as citric acid). Put a large pinch into the palm of your hand. With your other hand pick up a few drops of water from the faucet. Rub hands together until all the powder is dissolved and dispensed. It may sting briefly. Do this at bedtime, especially for cracked, chapped hands. Include lips if they need it.

50% Glycerin. Dilute 100% vegetable glycerin with an equal amount of water. This is useful as an after shave lotion.

Vitamin C liquid. Mix ¼ tsp. vitamin C powder in one pint water (opened capsules will do). This is useful as an after-shave lotion and general skin treatment.

Cornstarch. Use on rashes, fungus, moist or irritated areas and to prevent chafe.

Combining several of these makes them more effective.

Dry skin has several causes: too much water contact, too much soap contact (switch to borax), low body temperature, not enough fat in the diet, or parasites.

Massage Oil

Instead of using ANY oil, which may be benzene polluted, make yourself a cornstarch solution:
- **4 tsp. cornstarch**
- **1 cup water**

Boil starch and water until clear, about one minute.

Sunscreen Lotion

Purchase PABA in 500 mg tablet form. Dissolve 1 tablet in grain alcohol. Grind the tablet first by putting it in a plastic bag and rolling over it with a glass jar. It will not completely dissolve even if you use a tablespoon of the alcohol. Pour the whole mixture into a 4-ounce bottle of homemade skin softener. Be careful not to get the lotion into your eyes when applying it. A better solution is to wear a hat or stay out of the sun.

Nose Salve

(When the inside of the nose is dry, cracked and bleeding) Pour ½ tsp. pure vegetable glycerin into a bottle cap. Add ½ tsp. of water. To apply, use a plastic coffee stirrer or straw. Cut a slit in the end to catch some cotton wool salvaged from a vitamin bottle and twist (cotton swabs, cotton balls and wooden toothpicks are contaminated with 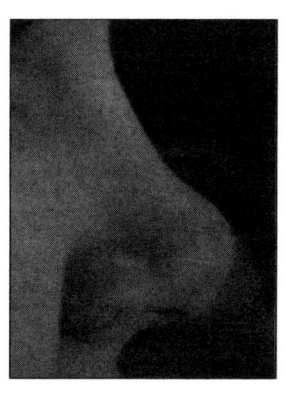 mercury, which in turn is polluted with thallium). Dip it into the glycerin mixture and apply inside the nose with a rotating motion. Do each nostril with a new applicator.

Quick Cornstarch Skin Softener

- 4 tsp. cornstarch
- 1 cup water

Boil starch and water until clear, about one minute.

Cornstarch Skin Softener

- 3 tsp. pure cornstarch
- 1 cup water
- 1 tsp. Vitamin C powder (ascorbic acid); or 5 capsules, 1000 mg each

Boil starch and water until clear, about one minute. Add vitamin C and stir until dissolved. Cool. Pour into dispenser bottle. Keep refrigerated when not in use.

After Shaves

Vitamin C. ¼ tsp. vitamin C powder, dissolved in 1 pint water.
Vegetable glycerin. Equal parts glycerin and water or to suit yourself.

Personal Lubricants

Heat these together: 1 level tsp. sodium alginate and 1 cup water in a covered non-metal pan until completely dissolved. Use very low heat and stir with a wooden spoon handle. It takes a fairly long time to get it perfectly smooth. After cooling, pour into a small dispenser bottle. <u>Keep refrigerated</u>.

Or, boil 4 tsp. cornstarch and 1 cup water until completely dissolved in a covered saucepan. Use non-metal dishes and a non-metal stirring spoon. Cool. Pour some into dispenser bottle. Keep refrigerated. This is many people's favorite recipe.

Baby Wipes

Cut paper towels in quarters and stack in a closeable plastic box. Run tap water over them; drain the excess. Add 1 tsp. grain alcohol and/or borax liquid on top. Close. Put a dab of the Quick Cornstarch Softener recipe on top of each wipe as you use it.

People Wipes

- ¼ tsp. powdered lysine
- ¼ tsp. vitamin C powder (you may open capsules)
- ¼ cup vegetable glycerin
- 1 cup water

Prepare wipes by cutting paper towels in quarters. Use white, unfragranced towels that are strong enough to hold up for this use. Fold each piece in quarters again and stack in a plastic zippered baggy. Pour the fluid mixture over the stack and zip. Store a bag full in the freezer to take on car trips. If you want to keep them a month or more, add 1 tbs. grain alcohol to the recipe.

For bathroom use, dampen a roll of paper towels under the cold tap first. Then pour about ¼ cup of the mixture over the towel roll around the middle. Store in a plastic shopping bag.

Natural Cosmetic Recipes

Eyeliner and Eyebrow Pencil

Get a pure charcoal pencil (black only) at an art supply store. Try several on yourself (bring a small mirror) in the store to see what hardness suits you. You may need to wet it with water or a vitamin E perle first. Don't put any chemicals on your *eyelids*, since this penetrates into your eye. To check this out for yourself, close your eye tightly and then dab lemon juice on your eyelid. It will soon burn! Everything that is put on skin penetrates. Otherwise the nicotine patch and estrogen patch wouldn't work. Not even soap belongs on your eyelids! Charcoal pencils are cheap. Get yourself half a dozen different kinds so you can do different things.

You could also use a capsule of activated charcoal. Empty it into a saucer. Mix glycerin and water, half and half, and add it to the charcoal powder until you get the consistency you like. Use a brush for eyelashes; use a finger for eyebrows.

Lipstick

- **Beet root powder**
- **100% vegetable glycerin**

Combine 1 tsp. vegetable glycerin and 1 tsp. beet root powder in a saucer. Stir until perfectly smooth. Then add ½ tsp. of vitamin E oil. Snip open vitamin E capsules or buy vitamin E oil. Very thick olive oil can be substituted. Apply liberally with your finger or a lipstick brush. Do not purse or rub your lips together after application. To make the lipstick stay on longer, apply 1 layer of lipstick, then dab some cornstarch over the lips, then apply another layer of lipstick. Store in a small glass or plastic container in the refrigerator, tightly covered in a plastic bag.

Face Powder

Use cornstarch from the original box. You may also try arrowroot starch or potato starch. Use your fingers or a tissue to apply because applicators can carry bacteria.

Blush

(face powder in a cake form)

Add 50% glycerin to cornstarch in a saucer to make a paste. Slowly add beet root powder to the desired color. To darken it try part of a charcoal capsule. A drop of food grade alcohol will also darken it. To make 50% glycerin, add equal parts of glycerin and water. Try to make the consistency the same as your brand name product, and you can even put it back in your brand name container.

Household Product Recipes

Floor Cleaner

Use washing soda from the grocery store. You may add borax and boric acid (to deter insects except ants). Use white distilled vinegar in your rinse water for a natural shine and ant repellent. Do not add bleach to this. Never use chlorine bleach if anybody in the home is ill or suffers from depression. Use grain alcohol (1 pint to 3 quarts water) for germ killing action instead of chlorine.

Furniture Duster & Window Cleaner

Mix equal parts white distilled vinegar and water. Put it in a spray bottle.

Furniture Polish

Put a few drops of olive oil on a dampened cloth. Use filtered water to dampen.

Insect Killer

Use boric acid powder (not borax). Throw liberal amounts behind stove, refrigerator, under carpets and in carpets. Since boric acid is white, you must be careful not to mistake it for sugar accidentally. Keep it far away from food and out of children's reach. Buy it at a farm supply or garden store). It will not kill ants.

Ant Repellent

Spray 50% white distilled vinegar on counter tops, windowsills and shelves and wipe, leaving residue. Start early in spring before they arrive, because it takes a few weeks to rid yourself of them once they are established. If you want immediate action, get some lemons, cut the yellow outer peel off and cover with grain alcohol in a tightly closed jar. Let stand at least one hour. Use 1 part of this concentrate with 9 parts water in a spray bottle. Mix only as much as you will use because the diluted form loses potency. Spray walls, floors, carpets wherever you see them. The lemon solution even leaves a shine on your counters. Use both vinegar and lemon approaches to rid yourself of ants.

To treat the **whole house**, pour vinegar all around your foundation, close to the wall, using one gallon for every five feet. Expect to damage any foliage it touches. Reapply every six months.

Flower & Foliage Spray

Use food-grade hydrogen peroxide. See instructions on bottle.

Herbal Moth Ball Substitute

I found this recipe in an old recipe book. Mix the following and scatter in trunks and bags containing furs and woolens: ½ lb. each rosemary and mint, ¼ lb. each tansy and thyme, 2 tbs. powdered Cloves .

Carpet Cleaner

Whether you rent a machine or have a cleaning service, <u>don't use the carpet shampoo they want to sell</u>, even if they "guarantee" that it is all natural and safe. Instead add these to a bucket (about four gallons) of water and use it as the cleaning solution:

- **Wash water**
- **$1/3$ cup borax**
- **¼ cup grain alcohol**
- **2 tsp. boric acid**
- **¼ cup white distilled vinegar or**
- **4 tsp. citric acid**
- **1 bottle povidone iodine (optional)**

Borax does the cleaning; alcohol disinfects, boric acid leaves a pesticide residue, and the vinegar or citric acid give luster. Povidone iodine kills parasite eggs. If you are just making one pass on your carpet, use the borax, alcohol, boric acid, and iodine. Remember to test everything you use on an unnoticed piece of carpet first.

Sources

Baking soda	Karlin Foods Corp., Spectrum Chemical Co., Self Health Resource Center
Barley flakes	Bob's Red Mill, Dutch Valley Foods
Bleach, USP ((NSF) also see Dental Bleach	Smart and Final; Wal-Mart; Target and others; Colgate Palmolive; Arctic White; Hilex, Javex
Birch bark tea	San Francisco Herb & Natural Food Co.
Black cherry concentrate	Bernard Jensen Products; health food store
Blender	Proctor-Silex; Wal-Mart; Target and others
Bottled water (kosher)	Acadia (distributed by Foodhold USA); Niagara Bottling LLC; Whistler Water Co.
Bread maker (no Teflon)	Breadman (Ultimate Plus), available – Target; Wal-Mart
Cleaning sponges	Scotch-Brite (Heavy-Duty 3M); U.F.O., Inc.; grocery store
Coffee mill (hand grinder)	Lehman's
Currants	Sun-Maid
Detergent- dishes	Colgate Palmolive (green bottle)
Detergent- dishwasher, liquid, no chlorine	Cascade
Detergent- dry, no chlorine	Cheer (*Free & Gentle*); Gain (*Island Fresh*); Ultra Tide 2X; Bold; Dona Blanca (Mexico)-should have no blue or green granules or powder
Essential Oils	Starwest Botanicals, Inc., Self Health Resource Center

Eucalyptus leaf, organic	San Francisco Herb & Natural Food Co.
Fennel	San Francisco Herb & Natural Food Co.
freezer chest (Whirlpool)	Costco; Sears
Ginger capsules	San Francisco Herb & Natural Food Co. (bulk)
Goat milk, butter, cheese	Meyenberg Dairy, health food stores
Good food (free of chlorine bleach)	Summer Kitchen (flour, tapioca perles, tapioca starch, currants, Demerara sugar, noodles [white & organic whole wheat], potato starch, arrowroot flour, raw pumpkin seeds, barley flakes, Red Star yeast)
Good grains	Bob's Red Mill (test to be sure)
Green Black Walnut Hull freeze-dried capsules	Health In-Sync ;New Action Products; Self Health Resource Center
Green Black Walnut Hull tincture	Health In-Sync ;New Action Products; Self Health Resource Center
Hair Dye, Black Walnut Hull (powder), Light Golden Blonde Medium Brown	San Francisco Herb & Natural Food Co. (Item #P246) Light Mountain Natural
hair dye (NOUR), pure black, Henna red	Karabetian Import; San Francisco Herb & Natural Food Co; Self Health Resource Center
Herbs, in bulk	San Francisco Herb & Natural Food Co.
Hydrangea (herb)	San Francisco Herb & Natural Food Co.
Juniper Berry Oil	Nature's Herb Co. (kosher and parve)
Maple Syrup	product of Canada or other foreign country; US Foods
Meat (Kosher)	S'Better Farms
Noodles (Amish made or Kosher))	Dutch Valley Foods
Nutmeg	San Francisco Herb & Natural Food Co.

Olive Oil	Bertolli Classico; Bertolli Extra Light; East Coast Olive Oil Corp.; Self Health Resource Center
Oregano oil	Starwest Botanicals, Inc.; North American Herb & Spice Co.
Paper towels	Kleenex Jumbo; Marathon; Max Soft (Mexico)
Peanut Butter	Laura Scudder's, Wild Oats
Peppermint leaf	San Francisco Herb & Natural Food Co.
Peppermint oil	Starwest Botanicals, Inc.
Pomegranate seeds, fresh (grind yourself); pomegranate peel capsules	San Francisco Herb & Natural Food Co. (for peel); Self Health Resource Center
Reishi mushroom	San Francisco Herb & Natural Food Co.
Rose hips	San Francisco Herb & Natural Food Co.
Salt (sodium chloride)	Spectrum Chemical Co.
Salt (sodium-potassium)	Self Health Resource Center
Shampoo	Perla
Soap, homemade	See *Recipes*; Self Health Resource Center; see individual ingredients
Stainless steel cookware	Restaurant supply stores, department stores – 18/10 quality (still must test)
Stainless steel platters	Tableware International Inc.
Stevia powder, extract	Self Health Resource Center
Strainer, stainless steel	San Francisco Herb & Natural Food Co.; Self Health Resource Center
Sucrose	Spectrum Chemical Co. (#SU103, Crystal, N.F.)
Sugar (raw)	Dutch Valley Foods
Tea ball, stainless steel	San Francisco Herb & Natural Food Co.; Self Health Resource Center
Toilet paper	Kirkland (Costco brand)
Toothbrush, slender style	Nutramax Products, Inc.; Drug and grocery store

HEALTHY RECIPES 142

Unchlorinated bottled water (*This is not an endorsement of bottled waters*)	Buhl; kosher
Vinegar (rice)	Mitsukan Rice Vinegar (no need to freeze; it has no bacteria); white vinegar for hair and cleaning – Herdez (Mexico)
wormwood capsules, mixture	Health In-Sync; New Action Products; San Francisco Herb & Natural Food Co.; Self Health Resource Center
Yeast for bread making	Bob's Red Mill; Red Star; Self Health Resource Center; Industria Mexicana de Alimentos S.A. de C.V.

Acadia Natural Spring Water
Landover, MD 20785
(877) 846-9949

Arizona Natural Products, Inc.
9849 N. 19th Dr., #3
Phoenix, AZ 85021
(800) 255-2823
www.arizonanatural.com

Bernard Jensen Products
535 Stevens Ave.
Solana Beach, CA 92075
(800) 755-4027
www.bernardjensen.org

Bertolli
www.bertolli.com

Blessed Herbs
109 Barre Plaines Rd.
Oakham, MA 01068
(508) 882-3839
(800) 489-4372
www.blessedherbs.com

Bob's Red Mill
5209 SE International Way
Milwaukie, OR 97222
(800) 349-2173
Fax (503) 653-1339
www.bobsredmill.com

Boiron Borneman
6 Campus Blvd.
Newtown Square, PA 19073
(800) 258-8823
(610) 325-7464
www.boiron.com

HEALTHY RECIPES

Bosworth Company
7227 N. Hamlin Ave.
Skokie, IL 60076
(800) 323-4352
www.bosworth.com

Breadman
www.bread-maker.net

Brushy Mountain Bee Farm
(800) 233-7929
www.beeequipment.com

Buhl Water Co.
(218) 258-3258
www.buhl-water.com

Consumer Health
Organization of Canada
1220 Sheppard Ave. E
Ste. 412
Toronto, Ontario M2K 2S5
CANADA
(416) 490-0986
www.consumerhealth.org

Dr. Clark Store
EUROPE
www.drclarkstore.eu

Dutch Valley Food
Distributors Inc.
PO Box 465
7615 Lancaster Ave.
Myerstown, PA 17067
www.dutchvalleyfoods.com

East Coast Olive Oil Corp.
75 Wurz Ave.
Utica, NY 13502
(351)797-7070
Fax (315) 797-6981
www.gem-ecoo.com

Health In-Sync
82 Oakwood Ave., Apt. #1
Toronto M6H2V8
CANADA
(416) 658-6125
Fax (416) 658-4140
www.healthinsync.com

Henry's Market place
www.wildoats.com

Karabetian Import
2450 Crystal St.
Los Angeles, CA 90039
(323) 664-8956
Fax (323) 664-8958
www.karabetian.com

Karlin Foods Corp.
1845 Oak St., Ste. 19
Winnetka, IL
(847) 441-8330
www.karlinfoods.com

Laura Scudder's
The J.M. Smucker Company
1 Strawberry Lane
Orrville, Ohio 44667-0280
(888) 550-9555
Fax: (330) 684-6410
www.laurascudderspeanutbutter.com

Lehman's
(888) 438-5346
www.lehmans.com

Light Mountain Natural
(800) 742-5841
www.bytheplanet.com

Mitsukan
www.mizkan.com

Mother Nature
322 7th Ave., 3rd Floor
New York, NY 10001
(800) 439-5506
Fax (212) 279-4290
www.mothernature.com

Meyenberg Dairy
(800) 891-GOAT
fax (209) 668-4977
www.myenberg.com

Nature's Alchemy
PO Box 489
Twin Lakes, WI 53181
(800) 905-6887
Toll Free (262) 889-8591
www.naturesalchemy.com

Nature's Herb Co.
410 Washington St.
Salisbury, MD 21804
www.herbalhut.com

New Action Products
PO Box 540
Orchard Park, NY 14127
(800) 455-6459 (USA only)
(716) 662-8000
USA

New Action Products
PO Box 141
Grimsby, Ontario
(800) 541-3799
(716) 873-3738
www.newactionproducts.com
CANADA

New Century Press
(Book Publisher)
1055 Bay Blvd., Ste. C
Chula Vista, CA 91911
(800) 519-2465
www.newcenturypress.com

Niagara Bottling, LLC
Irvine, CA 92614
(877) 487-7873
www.niagarawater.com

North American Herb &
Spice Co.
PO Box 4885
Buffalo Grove, IL 60089
(800) 243-5242
www.internatural-
alternative-health.com

Nutramax
51 Blackburn Dr.
Gloucester, MA 01930-2239
(978) 282-1800
Fax (978) 282-3794
www.nutamaxproducts.com

Healthy Recipes 145

Proctor-Silex
USA: (877) 474-1122
(800) 851-8900
CANADA: (800) 267-2826
MEXICO: 01 800 71 16 100
www.proctor-silex.com

Pure Water Products, LLC
10332 Park View Ave.
Westminster, CA 92683
(800) 478-7987
Box 2783
Denton, TX 76202
(940) 382-3814

R.H. Shumway
PO Box 1
Graniteville, SC 29829
(803) 663-9771
www.rhshumway.com

S'Better Farms
www.sbetterfarms.com

San Francisco Herb &
Natural Food Co.
47444 Kato Rd.
Fremont, CA 94538
(800) 227-2830 wholesale
(510) 770-1215 retail
www.herbspicetea.com

Scotch-Brite
3M Home Care Division
PO Box 33068
St. Paul, MN 55133

Self Heath Resource Center
1055 Bay Blvd. Suite A
Chula Vista, CA 91911
(800) 873-1663
www.shrc.net

Seltzer Chemicals, Inc.
5927 Geiger Ct.
Carlsbad, CA 92008-7305
(800) 735-8137
(760) 438-0089
Fax (760) 438-0336
www.nutritionaloutlook.com

Smart and Final
www.smartandfinal.com

Source of Health, Inc.
PO Box 161080
San Diego, CA 92176
(866) 372-5275
Fax (619) 795-0569

Spectrum Chemical Co.
14422 South San Pedro St.
Gardena, CA 90248
(800) 791-3210
(310) 516-8000
www.spectrumchemical.com

Starwest Botanicals, Inc.
11253 Trade Center Dr.
Rancho Cordova, CA 95742
(800) 273-4372
(916) 638-8100
www.starwestherb.com

HEALTHY RECIPES

Summer Kitchen
13110 Emerson Rd.
PO Box 221
Kidron, Ohio 44636
(866) 748-8500
Fax (330) 698-0413
www.summerkitchenonline.com

Sun-Maid
www.sunmaid.com

Tableware International Inc.
770 12th Ave.
San Diego, CA 92101
(619) 236-0210
Fax (619) 236-0130
Tableware@pacbell.net
www.internationaltableware.com

Target
www.target.com

The Natural Health Choice, Ltd.
44 292 055 4943
Fax 44 292 055 3779
www.the-natural-choice.co.uk

US Foods
www.usfoodservice.com

Wal-Mart
www.walmart.com

Whistler Water, Inc.
(604) 606-1903
www.whistlerwater.com